PUBLISHER COMMENTARY

There is a reason the U.S. Air Force has one of the best cyberwarfare **weapon system** programs.

This Air Force Instruction (AFI), developed in conjunction with other governing directives, prescribes procedures for operating the Network Attack System (NAS) under most circumstances. It covers cybercrew training and certification requirements, standard operating procedures, crew manning, crew duties, operational objectives, mission planning and preparation, mission go/no-go criteria, sortie duration, maintaining mission and Master Station Logs, required equipment, communications and crew coordination, and debrief guidance. Also discussed is the evaluation criteria for qualifying cybercrew members in the Network Attack System.

This publication pulls together the 3 volumes of AFI 17-2NAS Network Attack System (NAS).

AFI 17-2NAS Vol. 1	NETWORK ATTACK SYSTEM (NAS) TRAINING	10 Feb 2017
AFI 17-2NAS Vol. 2	NETWORK ATTACK SYSTEM (NAS) STANDARDIZATION AND EVALUATION	10 Feb 2017
AFI 17-2NAS Vol. 3	NETWORK ATTACK SYSTEM (NAS) OPERATIONS AND PROCEDURES	10 Feb 2017

These documents establish procedures for developing, distributing, evaluating and using Air Force training products for qualification training. They provide DoD approved baseline cybersecurity certifications requirements and workforce metrics for all levels of the military and civilian occupational series – Basic Cyber Qualified (BCQ), Basic Mission Capable (BMC), Mission Ready (MR)/Combat Mission Ready (CMR) – as well as continuation training requirements. Topics covered include network security and control systems training, network defense and defense analysis training, and network attack training.

Why buy a book you can download for free? We print this so you don't have to.

Some documents are only distributed in <u>electronic media</u>. Some online docs are missing some pages or the graphics are barely legible. When a new standard is released, an engineer prints it out, punches holes and puts it in a 3-ring binder. While this is not a big deal for a 5 or 10-page document, many cyber documents are over 100 pages and printing a large document is a time-consuming effort. So, an engineer that's paid $75 an hour is spending hours simply printing out the tools needed to do the job. That's time that could be better spent doing engineering. We publish these documents so engineers can focus on what they were hired to do – engineering.

A list of **Cybersecurity Standards** we publish is attached at the end of this document.

BY ORDER OF THE
SECRETARY OF THE AIR FORCE

AIR FORCE INSTRUCTION 17-2NAS
VOLUME 1

10 FEBRUARY 2017

Cyberspace

NETWORK ATTACK SYSTEM (NAS)
TRAINING

COMPLIANCE WITH THIS PUBLICATION IS MANDATORY

ACCESSIBILITY: Publications and forms are available for downloading or ordering on the e-Publishing website at www.e-publishing.af.mil.

RELEASABILITY: There are no releaseability restrictions on this publication.

OPR: AF/A3CO/A6CO

Certified by: AF/A3C/A6C
(Brig Gen Kennedy)
Pages: 25

This instruction implements Air Force (AF) Policy Directive (AFPD) 17-2, Cyberspace Operations, and Air Force Instruction (AFI) 17-202V1, *Cybercrew Training*. It establishes the minimum AF standards for training and qualifying/certifying personnel for performing crew duties on the Network Attack System (NAS) weapon system. This publication applies to all military and civilian AF personnel, members of the AF Reserve Command (AFRC), Air National Guard (ANG), third-party governmental employee and contractor support personnel in accordance with appropriate provisions contained in memoranda support agreements and AF contracts. The authorities to waive wing/unit level requirements in this publication are identified with a Tier ("T-0, T-1, T-2, T-3") number following the compliance statement. See AFI 33-360, Publications and Forms Management, Table 1.1 for a description of the authorities associated with the Tier numbers. This instruction requires collecting and maintaining information protected by the Privacy Act of 1974 (5 U.S.C. 552a). System of Records Notices F036 AF PC C, Military Personnel Records System, and OPM/GOVT-1, General Personnel Records, apply. When collecting and maintaining information protect it by the Privacy Act of 1974 authorized by 10 U.S.C. 8013. Ensure that all records created as a result of processes prescribed in this publication are maintained in accordance with AF Manual (AFMAN) 33-363, Management of Records, and disposed of in accordance with the AF Records Disposition Schedule (RDS) located in the AF Records Information Management System (AFRIMS). Units may supplement this instruction. All supplements will be coordinated through Headquarters (HQ) AFSPC/A2/3/6T prior to publication. Process supplements as shown in AFI 33-360, *Publications and Forms Management*. Major Command (MAJCOM) supplements will be coordinated with AF A3C/A6C. Guidance provided in weapon system-specific Instructions will contain specific training requirements unique to individual and crew positions. Send recommended changes or comments to HQ USAF/A3C/A6C, 1480 Air Force Pentagon, Washington, DC 20330-1480, through appropriate channels, using AF Form 847, *Recommendation for Change of Publication*. See Attachment 1 for a glossary of references and supporting information.

Chapter 1

GENERAL GUIDANCE

1.1. General. This instruction prescribes basic policy and guidance for training NAS crew members according to AFI 17-202 Volume 1, *Cybercrew Training*. The overall objective of the NAS training program is to develop and maintain a high state of readiness for the immediate and effective employment of the system across a full range of military options. Mission readiness and effective employment are achieved through the development and mastery of core competencies for NAS crew members.

1.2. References, Abbreviations, Acronyms and Terms. See Attachment 1.

1.2.1. For the purposes of this instruction, "certification" denotes a commander's action, whereas qualification denotes a formal Stan/Eval evaluation.

1.2.2. Key words explained.

1.2.2.1. "Will" or "shall" indicates a mandatory requirement.

1.2.2.2. "Should" indicates a preferred, but not mandatory, method of accomplishment.

1.2.2.3. "May" indicates an acceptable or suggested means of accomplishment.

1.2.2.4. "Note" indicates operating procedures, techniques, etc. which are considered essential to emphasize.

1.2.2.5. "Normally" indicates under normal or usual conditions; as a rule.

1.3. Responsibilities.

1.3.1. Squadrons. The Squadron (SQ)/CCs training priority will be to train all designated crew members to Combat Mission Ready (CMR). See paragraph 1.5.6 for CMR definitions and requirements. Squadron supervision will:

1.3.1.1. Ensure the Squadron Training Manager (SQ/DOT) is maintaining training forms and documents in Patriot Excalibur (or other suitable system) for all squadron personnel and personnel attached to the squadron for cyberspace operations **(T-3)**.

1.3.1.2. Oversee the implementation of a crew training documentation program for all unit-level personnel to ensure individual assigned and attached crew members are maintaining currencies, proficiencies, and requirements. **(T-3)**

1.4. Processing Changes. Process changes using the AF Form 847, in accordance with (IAW) AFI 33-360, through local and MAJCOM training channels to USAF/A3C/A6C for approval. **(T-3)**

1.5. Training. Crew training is designed to progress a crew member from IQT, or Requalification Training (RQT), to Mission Qualification Training (MQT) and finally to Continuation Training (CT). Upgrade Training is an additional training requirement to the NAS weapon system. **(T-3)**

1.5.1. Initial Qualification Training (IQT). Basic weapon-system training designed to cover system specific and/or positional specific training. IQT is a minimum requirement for entering MQT. IQT will be conducted during formal syllabus courses at the Formal Training Unit (FTU). See **Chapter 2**.

1.5.2. Mission Qualification Training (MQT). Unit-developed training program that upgrades IQT-complete crew members to CMR status to accomplish the unit Designated Operational Capability (DOC) statement mission. See **Chapter 3**.

1.5.3. Continuation Training (CT). CT consists of two aspects. The first involves training in the basic skills necessary to ensure the safe operation of the weapon system. The second consists of specific mission-related training required to accomplish the unit's assigned missions.

1.5.4. Requalification Training (RQT). Training designed to provide the training necessary to requalify a crew member with an expired qualification evaluation or loss of currency exceeding 6 months.

1.5.5. Ready Cybercrew Program (RCP). RCP is a CT program designed to focus training on capabilities needed to accomplish a unit's core tasked missions, fulfill DOC statement mission requirements, and/or provide focus on mission sets as determined by the SQ/CC. Upon completion of IQT and MQT, crew members will have received training in all the basic mission-sets of the unit. After MQT completion, crew members will then be assigned to a CMR manning position within the unit.

1.5.6. Combat Mission Ready (CMR). CMR is a status that denotes a crew member has satisfactorily completed IQT and MQT, and maintains certification, currency and proficiency in the command or unit combat mission.

1.5.6.1. All Crew Position Indicator (CPI)-1/-2/-A/-Z designated positions, to include SQ/CC and SQ/DO positions, should maintain CMR status. The Operations Group (OG)/CC may designate other CPI-6/B positions not assigned to the squadron as CMR. See Attachment 3 for CPI explanation and definitions.

1.5.6.2. CMR crew members will maintain currencies that affect CMR status, accomplish all core designated training (missions and events), and all mission related training. Failure to complete required CMR training or maintain currencies could result in regression to supervised status unless waived by the approval authority. **(T-3)**

1.5.7. Basic Mission Capable (BMC). There are no BMC positions associated with the NAS.

1.5.8. Specialized Training. Specialized training is any special skill(s) necessary to carry out the unit's assigned mission that is not required by every crew member.

1.5.8.1. Specialized training is normally accomplished after a crew member is assigned CMR status and is normally in addition to CMR requirements.

1.5.8.2. SQ/CCs will determine and assign crew members that will train for and maintain special mission certification/qualification. **(T-3)**

1.6. Training Concepts and Policies. Units will design training to achieve the highest degree of readiness consistent with safety and resource availability. Training must balance the need for realism against the expected threat, crew capabilities, and safety. This volume provides training guidelines and polices for use with operational procedures specified in applicable operational publications.

1.6.1. Design training to achieve mission capability in squadron-tasked roles, maintain proficiency, and enhance mission accomplishment and safety. RCP training missions should emphasize either basic combat skills, or scenarios that reflect procedures and operations based on employment plans, location, current intelligence, and opposition capabilities. Use of procedures and actions applicable to mission scenarios is desired. **(T-3)**

1.7. Experienced Crew Requirements. NAS crew members are declared experienced on the weapon system when they achieve the following:

1.7.1. NAS Crew Commander: 540 hours in the NAS weapon system. **(T-3)**

1.7.2. NAS Operations Controller: 540 hours in the NAS weapon system. **(T-3)**

1.7.3. NAS Operator: 540 hours in the NAS weapon system. **(T-3)**

1.8. RCP Policy and Management.

1.8.1. The RCP training cycle is each fiscal year and executed IAW the RCP Tasking Memorandum (RTM). RCP CT status is defined by a total number of RCP missions, broken down into mission types, plus specific qualifications and associated events as determined by higher headquarters (HHQ) guidance and unit commanders.

1.8.2. The total number of RCP missions is the primary factor for maintaining an individual's CT status. The breakout of mission types is provided as a guideline to be followed as closely as possible but minor variances are authorized. Variations in mission types may be used as a basis for regression as directed by the SQ/CC or SQ/DO. **(T-3)**

1.8.3. An effective RCP training mission requires accomplishing a tactical mission profile or a building block type mission. Each mission requires successfully completing a majority of the applicable events, as determined by the SQ/CC or SQ/DO. **(T-3)**

1.9. Training Mission Program Development.

1.9.1. RTM mission and event requirements apply to all NAS crew members as well as those carrying special mission certifications/qualifications. The standard mission requirements listed in the RTM establish the minimum number of missions per training cycle. The RTM takes precedence over this volume and may contain updated requirements, missions, events, or tasks not yet incorporated into the standard NAS mission profile. **(T-3)**

1.9.2. Non-effective sorties are logged when a training sortie is planned and started, but 50% of valid training for that type of mission is not accomplished due to system malfunction, power failures, etc. Non-effective sorties will be logged and reported appropriately. **(T-3)**

1.10. Training Records and Reports.

1.10.1. Units will maintain crew records for individual training and evaluations IAW:

1.10.1.1. AFI 17-202V1, *Cybercrew Training.*

1.10.1.2. AFI 17-202V2, *Cybercrew Standardization & Evaluation.*

1.10.1.3. Any additional HHQ supplement to the above mentioned volumes.

1.10.2. Track the following information for all crew members (as applicable):

1.10.2.1. Mission-related training (e.g., tactics training, crew resource management training, etc.). **(T-3)**

1.10.2.2. Requirements and accomplishment of individual training or requalification training. **(T-)**

1.10.2.3. Currencies.

1.11. Crew Utilization Policy.

1.11.1. Commanders will ensure wing/group crew members (CPI-1/-2/-A/-Z) fill authorized positions IAW UMDs and that crew member status is properly designated (see Attachment 3 for CPI explanation and definitions). The overall objective is for crew members to perform mission-related duties. Supervisors may assign crew members to valid, short-term tasks (escort officer, operational review board (ORB), etc.), but must continually weigh the factors involved, such as level of tasking, proficiency, currency, and experience. Supervisors should limit non-crew duties for inexperienced crew members in the first year of their initial operational assignment to those related to unit mission activities. **(T-3)**

1.11.2. Use evaluators as instructors for any phase of training for which they are qualified to capitalize on their expertise and experience. If an evaluator is an individual's primary or recommending instructor, the same evaluator shall not administer the associated evaluation. **(T-3)**

1.12. Sortie Allocation and Unit Manpower Guidance.

1.12.1. In general, inexperienced CPI-1/-2/-A/-Z crew members should receive priority over experienced crew members. Priorities for sortie allocation are as follows:

1.12.1.1. Operational Units. CMR CPI-1/-2/-A/-Z, MQT CPI-1/-2/-A/-Z, CMR CPI-6/-8/-B/-D, MQT CPI-6/-8/-B/-D. **(T-3)**

1.12.2. Units should provide assigned CPI-6/-8/-B/-D crew members adequate resources to maintain minimum training requirements. However, CPI-6/-8/-B/-D support will not come at the expense of the squadron's primary mission. **(T-3)**

1.12.3. If attached crew members cannot meet requirements, they must request relief/waiver from the OG/CC. **(T-3)**

1.12.4. There is no maximum sortie requirement for CMR crew members. The minimum sortie requirement for all crew positions is one (1) sortie every 30 days. **(T-3)**

1.13. Training on Operational Missions. Training during operational missions will be IAW unit Operating Instructions. **(T-3)**

1.14. In-Unit Training Time Limitations.

1.14.1. Comply with the time limitations in unit Operating Instructions. Crew members entered in an in-unit training program leading to qualification or requalification will be dedicated to that training program on a full-time basis. **(T-3)**

1.14.2. DOT will notify the SQ/CC (or designee) in writing before the crew member exceeds training time limits. SQ/CCs may extend listed training times up to 60 days provided appropriate documentation is included in the training folder. **(T-3)**

1.14.2.1. Include training difficulty, unit corrective action to resolve and prevent recurrence, and estimated completion date. **(T-3)**

Table 1.1. In-Unit Training Time Limitations (Calendar Days).

Training	Crew Commander	Operations Controller	Operator
Mission Qualification Training	60	90	60
Requalification	45	45	45
Position Upgrade	60	60	60

1.15. Periodic and End-of-Cycle Training Reports.

1.15.1. Periodic Reporting. Squadrons will submit a periodic training report to 67 COG/CC by the 5th day of every quarter during training cycle (if the 5th day falls on a weekend/holiday, then by the next business day). Reports will consist of a SQ/CC memo summarizing previous report results/issues, current training plan summary and significant shortfalls/limiting factors (LIMFACS) affecting training. **(T-3)**

1.15.2. End-of-Cycle Reporting. Squadrons will submit an End-of-Cycle Training Report NLT 5 October. Report all deviations from the training requirements in this volume or the RTM, after proration at the end of the training cycle. **(T-3)**

1.15.3. Reporting Formats. Report formats and additional reporting requirements will be specified in the 67 COG RTM. **(T-3)**

1.16. Waiver Authority.

1.16.1. Waiver authority for all requirements of the RTM is the OG/CC. Additional guidance may be provided in the memo. Unless specifically noted otherwise in the appropriate section, and also with AFSPC/A2/3/6 approval, the OG/CC may adjust individual requirements in **Chapter 4** and **Chapter 5**, on a case-by-case basis, to accommodate variations in crew experience and performance. **(T-3)**

1.16.2. Formal School Training and Prerequisites. Any planned exception to a formal course syllabus (or prerequisite) requires a syllabus waiver. Submit waiver request through AFSPC/A2/3/6T (or equivalent) or the waiver authority listed in the course syllabus. If required for units' designated mission, events waived or not accomplished at the formal school will be accomplished in-unit before assigning CMR status. **(T-2)**

1.16.3. In-Unit Training Waiver. AFSPC/A2/3/6T (or equivalent) is approval/waiver authority for in-unit training to include syllabus and prerequisite waivers. Before approval, review the appropriate syllabus and consider availability of formal instruction and requirements. All in-unit training will utilize formal courseware in accordance with AFI 17-202 Volume 1. AFSPC/A2/3/6T will coordinate with the FTU to arrange courseware delivery to the unit for in-unit training. **(T-2)**

1.16.4. Waiver authority for supplemental guidance will be as specified in the supplement and approved through higher level coordination authority. **(T-2)**

1.16.5. Units subordinate to a NAF will forward requests through the NAF/A3T to AFSPC/A2/3/6T.. AFSPC/A2/3/6T will coordinate all waiver requests with 24 AF/A3T. **(T-2)**

1.16.6. Unless specifically stated in the waiver, approval waivers to this volume will be valid until the approving official cancels the waiver in writing, the waiver expires, or this publication is revised to include waived requirements. Otherwise, waivers extending beyond the end of the annual training cycle must be re-submitted at the start of each subsequent training cycle. **(T-2)**

1.16.7. Waiver Format. Submit waiver requests using AF Form 679, *Air Force Publication Compliance Item Waiver Request/Approval* through OG/CC (or equivalent) to the appropriate MAJCOM OPR. Units will submit waiver requests according to Table 1.2. Place a copy of approved waivers in the individual's training folder. **(T-2)**

Table 1.2. Processing Waivers to AFI 17-2.NAS Volume 1.

If waiver is requested by:	Send waiver request to:	Waiver authority will send approval or disapproval to:	With information copies to:
Active Duty Cyberspace Wing or Group	MAJCOM/A3T	OG/CC	24 AF/A3T
FTU	AFSPC/A2/3/6T	OG/CC	24 AF/A3T
USAFWS	USAFWS/CO to AFSPC/A2/3/6T	USAFWS/CO	24 AF/A3T

Chapter 2

INITIAL QUALIFICATION TRAINING

2.1. General. This chapter outlines NAS IQT requirements for all crew members.

2.2. Formal Training. NAS IQT includes training that will be conducted during formal syllabus courses at the FTU.

2.3. Local Training. When FTU training is not available within a reasonable time period, local IQT may be performed at the unit IAW the provisions of this chapter. Local IQT will be conducted using appropriate formal training course syllabus and requirements. When local IQT is authorized, the gaining unit assumes responsibility for the burden of providing this training. **(T-2)**

2.3.1. Requests to conduct local IQT will include the following:

2.3.1.1. Justification for the local training in lieu of FTU training. **(T-2)**

2.3.1.2. Summary of individual's mission related experience, to include dates. **(T-2)**

2.3.1.3. Date training will begin and expected completion date. **(T-2)**

2.3.1.4. Requested exceptions to formal course syllabus, with rationale. **(T-2)**

2.4. Mission-Related Training. Mission-related training may be tailored to the individual's background and experience or particular local conditions. Current and available reference materials, such as AF Tactics, Techniques, and Procedures (AFTTP) 3-1.NAS, other applicable AFTTP 3-1s and 3-3s, unit guides, and other available training material and programs, will be used as supporting materials to the maximum extent possible. **(T-3)**

2.5. Mission Training.

2.5.1. Mission sequence and prerequisites will be IAW the appropriate formal course syllabus (unless waived). **(T-2)**

2.5.2. Training will be completed within the time specified by the syllabus. Failure to complete within the specified time limit requires notification through channels to MAJCOM/A3 with crew member's name, rank, reason for delay, planned actions, and estimated completion date. **(T-2)**

2.5.3. Crew members in IQT will train under the appropriate supervision as annotated in the formal course syllabus until completing the QUAL evaluation. **(T-2)**

2.5.4. Formal course syllabus mission objectives and tasks are minimum requirements for IQT. However, additional training events, based on student proficiency and background, may be incorporated into the IQT program. Additional training due to student non-progression is available within the constraints of the formal course syllabus and may be added at SQ/CC discretion. **(T-3)**

2.6. IQT for Senior Officers.

2.6.1. All senior officer training (colonel selects and above) will be conducted at the FTUs unless waived IAW AFI 17-202V1. **(T-2)**

2.6.2. Senior officers must meet course entry prerequisites and will complete all syllabus requirements unless waived IAW AFI 17-202V1. **(T-2)**

2.6.3. If senior officers are trained at the base to which they are assigned they will be considered in a formal training status for the duration of the course. Their duties will be turned over to appropriate CDs or CVs until training is completed. Waiver authority for this paragraph is MAJCOM/CC (submitted through MAJCOM/A3). **(T-2)**

Chapter 3

MISSION QUALIFICATION AND CERTIFICATION TRAINING

3.1. General. MQT is a unit-developed training program that upgrades IQT-complete crew members to CMR status to accomplish the unit DOC statement missions. Guidance in this chapter, which represents the minimum, is provided to assist SQ/CCs in developing their MQT program, which must have OG/CC approval prior to use. Squadrons are allowed to further tailor their program for individual crew member, based on current qualifications (e.g., USAFWS graduate, Instructor), certifications (e.g., Mission Commander (MC), Defensive Counter-Cyber (DCC), Stan/Eval), experience, currency, documented performance, and formal training. Squadrons may use applicable portions of MQT to create a recertification program. **(T-3)**

3.1.1. MQT will be completed within 60 or 90 calendar days (depending on crew position) starting from the crew member's first duty day in the gaining unit. **(T-3)** If the crew member elects to take leave prior to being entered into MQT, the timing will begin after the termination of the leave. Training is complete upon SQ/CC certification of CMR status (subsequent to the successful completion of the MQT MSN qualification evaluation). Notify SQ/CC either if training exceeds the standard time period or there is a delay beginning MQT (e.g., due to security clearance) that exceeds 30 days. **(T-3)**

3.2. Mission-Related Training.

3.2.1. Units will develop blocks of instruction covering areas pertinent to the mission as determined by the SQ/CC. Training accomplished during IQT may be credited towards this requirement. **(T-3)**

3.2.2. Mission-related training may be tailored to the individual's background and experience or particular local conditions. Current and available reference materials, such as AFTTP 3-1.NAS, other applicable AFTTP 3-1s and 3-3s, unit guides, and other available training material and programs, will be used as supporting materials to the maximum extent possible. **(T-3)**

3.2.3. Mission-related training will be built to support the mission and concept of operations of the individual squadron; incorporate appropriate portions of AFTTP 3-1.NAS and other mission-related documents. **(T-3)**

3.3. Initial Certification.

3.3.1. Initial Certification of CMR crew position will be completed within 30 days after completing MQT IAW AFI 17-2NAS Volume 2 and unit Operating Instructions. **(T-3)**

3.4. Mission Training.

3.4.1. MQT programs should use profiles typical of squadron missions. **(T-3)**

3.4.2. Supervision. A SQ instructor is required for all training missions unless specified otherwise. **(T-3)**

3.4.3. Minimum Sortie Requirements. The minimum sorties required in a local MQT program will be IAW the MQT course syllabus (not required if portions of the MQT program are used to recertify crew members). **(T-3)**

3.4.4. Training will be completed within the time specified by the syllabus. **(T-2)**

3.4.5. Crew members in MQT will train under the appropriate supervision as annotated in the formal course syllabus until completing the MSN evaluation. **(T-3)**

3.5. MQT for Senior Officers.

3.5.1. All senior officer training (colonel selects and above) will be conducted at the unit. **(T-2)**

3.5.2. Senior officers must meet course entry prerequisites and will complete all syllabus requirements unless waived by the MAJCOM/A3. **(T-2)**

3.5.3. Senior officers will be considered in a formal training status for the duration of the course. Their duties will be turned over to appropriate CDs or CVs until training is completed. Waiver authority for this paragraph is the MAJCOM/CC (submitted through the MAJCOM/A3). **(T-2)**

Chapter 4

CONTINUATION TRAINING

4.1. General. This chapter establishes the minimum crew member training requirements to maintain CMR for an assigned training status. The SQ/CC will ensure each crew member receives sufficient training to maintain individual currency and proficiency. **(T-3)**

4.2. Crew Status. All NAS crew members must maintain CMR status. **(T-3)**

4.2.1. Combat Mission Ready (CMR). For Resource Readiness, a crew member who satisfactorily completed IQT and MQT, and maintains qualification, certification, currency and proficiency in the command or unit combat mission.

4.2.2. Non-Mission Ready (NMR). A crew member that is unqualified, non-current or incomplete in required continuation training, or not certified to perform the unit mission.

4.2.3. All crew members will accomplish and/or maintain RCP requirements, for their respective status, and the appropriate events in the RCP tables in this instruction and the RTM. **(T-3)**

4.3. Training Events/Tables. Standardized training events, identifiers, and descriptions are available at a higher classification. Units will include unit-specific events to include a description in their local training documentation. **(T-3)**

4.3.1. Crediting Event Accomplishment. Credit events accomplished on training, operational missions and satisfactory evaluations or certifications toward RCP requirements and establish a subsequent due date. Use date of successful evaluation as the date of accomplishment for all mission-related training events that were trained during a formal course. A successful evaluation establishes a new current and qualified reference date for all accomplished events. For training during IQT or requalification training, numbers of events accomplished prior to the evaluation are not credited to any crew position. In all cases, numbers of events successfully accomplished during the evaluation or certification are credited toward the crew position. **(T-3)**

4.3.2. For an unsatisfactory evaluation, do not log CT requirements for those events graded U/Q3 (according to AFI 17-202V2) until re-qualified. **(T-3)**

4.3.3. Instructors and evaluators may credit up to 50 percent of their total CT requirements while instructing or evaluating. **(T-3)**

4.4. Continuation Training Requirements. Completion and tracking of continuation training is ultimately the responsibility of the individual crew member. Crew members should actively work with their supervisors, unit schedulers and training offices to ensure accomplishment of their continuation training requirements. Crew members attached to units are responsible for reporting accomplished training event to their attached unit. **(T-3)**

4.5. Mission Training Events. Crew members will comply with requirements of the RTM for their respective position. Total sorties and events are minimums which ensure training to continually meet all DOC tasked requirements and may not be reduced except in proration/waiver. Upon AFSPC approval, the OG/CC is the waiver authority for all RCP requirements and for all provisions in Chapter 4 and Chapter 5 of this volume. Failure to accomplish events in these tables may lead to NMR status. **(T-3)**

4.6. Specialized Mission Training. Training in any special skills (e.g., tactics, weapon system capabilities, responsibilities, etc.) necessary to carry out the unit's assigned mission that is not required by every crew member.

4.7. Multiple Qualification/Currency. See AFI 17-202V1, AFI 17-202V2, applicable HHQ guidance, and AFI 17-2NAS V2 for multiple qualifications.

4.8. Currencies, Recurrency, and Requalification.

4.8.1. Currency. The RTM defines currency requirements for crew members. Crew members may not instruct, evaluate or perform any event in which they are not qualified and current unless under instructor supervision. Currency may be established or updated by:

4.8.1.1. Accomplishing the event as a qualified crew member provided member's currency has not expired. **(T-3)**

4.8.1.2. Accomplishing the event as a qualified crew member under supervision of a current instructor. **(T-3)**

4.8.1.3. Events satisfactorily performed on any evaluation may be used to establish or update currency in that event. **(T-3)**

4.8.2. If a crew member loses a particular currency, thereby requiring recurrency, that mission or event may not be performed except for the purpose of regaining currency. Noncurrent events must be satisfied before the crew member is considered certified/qualified (as applicable) to perform those events unsupervised. **(T-3)**

4.9. Loss of Instructor Status and Requalification/Recurrency. Instructors may lose instructor status for the following:

4.9.1. They become noncurrent in a mission or event.

4.9.1.1. If the SQ/CC does not elect to decertify the individual or if the individual becomes noncurrent in missions or events which do not require removal from CMR status, instructor status may be retained, but the instructor will not instruct that mission or event until the required currency is regained. **(T-3)**

4.9.2. Instructor Lack of Ability. Instructors serve solely at the discretion of the SQ/CC. Instructors should exemplify a higher level of performance and present themselves as reliable and authoritative experts in their respective duty positions. Instructors exhibiting substandard performance should be reviewed for suitability of continued instructor duty. Individuals will be removed from duty as instructors if **(T-3)**:

4.9.2.1. They are awarded a less than fully qualified grade in any area of the evaluation regardless of overall crew position qualification. **(T-3)**

4.9.2.2. They fail a qualification.

4.9.2.3. The SQ/CC deems the instructor is substandard, ineffective, or providing incorrect procedures, techniques, or policy guidance. **(T-3)**

4.9.3. Crew members may regain instructor status by correcting applicable deficiencies and completing the training as specified by the SQ/CC. **(T-3)**

4.10. Regression.

4.10.1. Failure to Meet Lookback. Only RCP training missions and cyberspace operations sorties may be used for lookback. Crew lookback requirements and policies will be IAW applicable unit Operating Instructions. **(T-3)**

4.10.1.1. Lookback computations begin following completion of MQT. SQ/CCs may apply probation rules IAW unit Operating Instructions. **(T-3)**

4.10.2. Failed Evaluations. Crew members who fail a periodic evaluation are unqualified and will regress to NMR. Crew members will remain NMR until successfully completing required corrective action, re-evaluation, are re-certified by the SQ/CC. **(T-3)**

4.10.3. Failure to Maintain Standards. If a qualified crew member demonstrates lack of proficiency or knowledge, the SQ/CC may elect to regress the individual to NMR. These crew members will remain NMR until successful completion of corrective action as determined by the SQ/CC, an evaluation if required and are re-certified by the SQ/CC. **(T-3)**

4.10.4. End of Cycle Requirements. Crew members who fail to complete sortie or event requirements by the end of training cycle may require additional training depending on the type and magnitude of the deficiency. In all cases, units will report training shortfalls to the OG/CC. **(T-3)**

4.11. Proration of Training.

4.11.1. Proration of End-of-Cycle Requirements. At the end of the training cycle the SQ/CC may prorate any training requirements precluded by the following events: initial arrival date in squadron, emergency leave, non-mission temporary duties (TDYs) (i.e., PME) or exercises, or deployments. Ordinary annual leave will not be considered as non-availability. Other extenuating circumstances, as determined by the SQ/CC, that prevent crew from mission duties for more than 15 consecutive days may be considered as non-availability for proration purposes. The following guidelines apply:

4.11.1.1. Proration will not be used to mask training or planning deficiencies. **(T-3)**

4.11.1.2. Proration is based on cumulative days of non-availability for mission duties in the training cycle. Use Table 4.1 to determine the number of months to be prorated based on each period of cumulative non-mission duty calendar days. **(T-3)**

4.11.1.3. If IQT or MQT is re-accomplished, a crew members training cycle will start over at a prorated share following completion of IQT/MQT. **(T-3)**

Table 4.1. Proration Allowance.

CUMULATIVE DAYS OF NON-MISSION ACTIVITY	PRORATION ALLOWED (Months)
0 – 15	0
16 – 45	1
46 – 75	2

76 – 105	3
106 – 135	4
136 – 165	5
166 – 195	6
196 – 225	7
226 – 255	8
256 – 285	9
286 – 315	10
316 – 345	11
Over 345	12

4.12. Operational Missions. Missions conducted during operational sorties count toward annual RCP requirements. **(T-3)**

4.13. Regaining CMR Status. If CMR status is lost, re-certification/re-qualification will be IAW unit Operating Instructions and at the discretion of the SQ/CC or SQ/DO. **(T-3)**

Chapter 5

UPGRADE AND SPECIALIZED MISSION TRAINING

5.1. General. This chapter outlines duties and responsibilities for units to upgrade, certify, and maintain currency/proficiency for special capabilities, and certifications/qualifications. SQ/CCs may tailor programs for individuals based on previous experience, qualifications, and documented performance. These capabilities and certifications/qualifications are in addition to unit core missions and do not apply to every crew member assigned or attached to the unit.

5.2. Requirements. Requirements for upgrade and special mission training are listed in unit Operating Instructions as well as on documentation at a higher classification level. Additionally, commanders must ensure each candidate has the ability, judgment, technical expertise, skill, and experience when selecting a crew member for upgrade or specialized mission training. **(T-3)**

5.3. Instructor Upgrade. This section establishes the minimum guidelines for instructor upgrade.

5.3.1. Instructor Responsibilities. An AF instructor shall be a competent subject matter expert adept in the methodology of instruction. The instructor shall be proficient in evaluating, diagnosing, and critiquing student performance, identifying learning objectives and difficulties, and prescribing and conducting remedial instruction. The instructor must be able to conduct instruction in all training venues (e.g., classroom, training devices, ops floor, mission execution, etc.) **(T-3)**

5.3.1.1. Instructor Prerequisites. SQ/CCs will consider ability, judgment, technical expertise, skill, and experience when selecting a crew member for instructor upgrade. **(T-3)**

5.3.1.2. For instructor minimum requirements, see Table 5.2. All instructor candidates will be CMR in their unit's mission. USAF Weapons School graduates are instructor qualified. **(T-3)**

Table 5.1. Instructor Upgrade Requirements (T-3).

Position	Instructor	Tasks/Events to Complete Upgrade	Notes
CCC-A	1000	Instructor Training Course	See Notes 1 & 2
OC-A	1000	Instructor Training Course	See Notes 1 & 2
CO-A	2000	Instructor Training Course	See Notes 1 & 2
OT-A	2000	Instructor Training Course	See Notes 1 & 2
Notes:			
1. Instructor training must meet all AFI 17-202 V1 and other HHQ guidance requirements.			
2. Award of the "K" prefix will be IAW AF Officer and Enlisted Classification Directories.			

5.3.1.3. Training. Instructor training should expand the instructor candidate's weapon-system subject matter expertise. Instructor training will include methodology of instruction and make instructor candidates proficient in evaluating, diagnosing, and critiquing student performance, identifying learning objectives and difficulties, and prescribing and conducting remedial instruction. The instructor candidate must be able to conduct instruction in all training venues (e.g., classroom, training devices, ops floor, mission execution, etc.). **(T-3)**

5.3.1.4. Qualifications and Certifications. All instructor candidates will demonstrate to an evaluator their ability to instruct and perform selected tasks and items IAW applicable directives.. They must demonstrate their ability to instruct and perform selected tasks and items according to applicable directives. SQ/CC will certify a new instructor by placing a letter of certification in the training folder and indicate qualifications on a letter of Xs forwarded to the 26th Operational Support Squadron (OSS)/OST. **(T-3)**

WILLIAM J. BENDER, Lt Gen, USAF
Chief of Information Dominance and
Chief Information Officer

Attachment 1

GLOSSARY OF REFERENCES AND SUPPORTING INFORMATION

References

AFI 17-202V1, *Cybercrew Training*, April 2, 2014

AFI 17-202V2, *Cybercrew Standardization and Evaluation Program*, October 15, 2014

AFI 33-360, Publications and Forms Management, 25 Sep 2013

Abbreviations and Acronyms

AF—Air Force

AFI—Air Force Instruction

AFMAN—Air Force Manual

AFPD—Air Force Policy Directive

AFRC—Air Force Reserve Command

AFRIMS—Air Force Records Information Management System

AFSPC—Air Force Space Command

AFTTP—Air Force Tactics, Techniques and Procedures

ANG—Air National Guard

BCQ—Basic Cyber Qualified

BMC—Basic Mission Capable

CC—Commander

CD—Deputy Commander

CMR—Combat Mission Ready

CPI—Crew Position Indicator

CT—Continuation Training

CV—Vice Commander

DCC – Defensive Counter—Cyber

DO—Director of Operations

DOC—Designed Operational Capability

DOT—Director of Operational Training/Squadron Training Function

FLT—Flight

FTU—Formal Training Unit

HQ—Headquarters

HHQ—Higher Headquarters

IAW—In Accordance With

IQT—Initial Qualification Training

LIMFAC—Limiting Factor

MAJCOM—Major Command

MC—Mission Commander

MQT—Mission Qualification Training

NAS—Network Attack System

NMR – Non—Mission Ready

OG—Operations Group

OPR—Office of Primary Responsibility

ORB—Operational Review Board

OSS—Operations Support Squadron

RDS—Records Disposition Schedule

RCP—Ready Cybercrew Program

RTM—RCP Tasking Memorandum

RQT—Requalification Training

SORTS—Status of Resources and Training

SQ—Squadron

TDY—Temporary Duty

USAF—United States Air Force

USAFWS—United States Air Force Weapons School

WG— Wing

WIC—Weapons Instructor Course

Terms

Additional Training—Any training recommended to remedy deficiencies identified during an evaluation that must be completed by a specific due date. This training may include self-study or simulator. Additional training must include demonstration of satisfactory knowledge or proficiency to examiner, supervisor or instructor (as stipulated in the Additional Training description) to qualify as completed.

Attached Personnel—This includes anyone not assigned to the unit but maintaining qualification through that unit. HAF augmented personnel are an example of attached personnel.

Basic Cyber Qualified (BCQ)—A crew member who has satisfactorily completed IQT. The crew member will carry BCQ only until completion of MQT. BCQ crew members will not perform RCP-tasked events or sorties without instructor crewmembers.

Basic Mission Capable (BMC)—A crew member who has satisfactorily completed IQT and MQT, but is not in fully-certified MR/CMR status. Crew member accomplishes training required to remain familiarized in all and may be qualified and proficient in some of the primary missions of their weapon system BMC requirements. These crew members may also maintain special mission qualification.

Certification—Designation of an individual by the certifying official (normally the SQ/CC) as having completed required training and being capable of performing a specific duty.

Continuation Training (CT)— Training which provides crew members with the volume, frequency, and mix of training necessary to maintain currency and proficiency in the assigned qualification level.

Currency—A measure of how frequently and/or recently a task is completed. Currency requirements should ensure the average crew member maintains a minimum level of proficiency in a given event.

Combat Mission Ready (CMR)—A crew member who has satisfactorily completed IQT and MQT, and maintains certifications, currency, and Proficiency in the command or unit combat mission.

Crew Position Indicator (CPI)—Codes used to manage crew positions to ensure a high state of readiness is maintained with available resources.

Cyberspace Operations (CO)—The employment of cyberspace capabilities where the primary purpose is to achieve objectives in or through cyberspace.

Experienced Crew (EXP)—Management term describing crew who meet the requirement as dictated per within the weapon system specific volumes.

Initial Qualification Training (IQT)—Weapon system-specific training designed to cover system specific and/or positional specific training leading to declaration of BCQ as a prerequisite to Mission Qualification Training (MQT).

Instructor—An experienced individual qualified to instruct other individuals in mission area academics and positional duties. Instructors will be qualified appropriately to the level of the training they provide.

Instructor Event—An event logged by an instructor when performing instructor duties during the sortie, or a portion thereof. Instructor qualification required and used for the mission or a mission element. Examples include upgrade sorties, updating lost currencies, etc. Instructors will log this event on evaluation sorties.

Lookback— A management tool used to determine and monitor CMR crew member proficiency during the training cycle. A crew member's lookback requirements are based on the crew member's experience status.

Mission—A set of tasks that lead to an objective, to include associated planning, brief, execution, and debrief.

Mission Qualification Training (MQT)—Following IQT, MQT is a formal training program used to qualify crew members in assigned crew positions to perform the unit mission. This training is required to achieve a basic level of competence in unit's primary tasked missions and is a prerequisite for MR/CMR or BMC declaration.

Non-effective Sortie—A sortie in which 50% of planned RCP events were not accomplished.

Proficiency—A measure of how well a task is completed. A crew member is considered proficient when they can perform tasks at the minimum acceptable levels of speed, accuracy, and safety.

Qualification (QUAL—) – Designation of an individual by the unit commander as having completed required training and evaluation and being capable of performing a specific duty.

Ready Cybercrew Program (RCP)—Annual sortie/event training requirements for crews to maintain mission ready/combat mission ready (MR/CMR) status.

Requalification Training (RQT)—Training required to recertify a crew member with an expired qualification evaluation or loss of currency exceeding 6 months.

Sortie—The actions an individual cyberspace weapon system takes to accomplish a mission and/or mission objective(s) within a defined start and stop period.

Specialized Mission Training—Training in any special skills (e.g., tactics, weapon system capabilities, responsibilities, etc.) necessary to carry out the unit's assigned missions that are not required by every crew member. Specialized training is normally accomplished after the crew member is assigned MR/CMR or BMC status, and is normally in addition to MR/CMR or BMC requirements. This training may require an additional certification and/or qualification event as determined by the SQ/CC.

Squadron Supervisor—May include all or some of the following depending on specific guidance and SQ/CC concurrence: SQ/CC, SQ/DO, ADOs, and FLT/CCs.

Supervisory Crew or Staff Member—Personnel in supervisory or staff positions (CPI-6/8/B/D) who actively conduct cyber operations.

Supervised Status—The status of a crew member who must perform mission under the supervision of an instructor.

Training Level—Assigned to individuals based on the continuation training status (basic cyber qualification, basic mission capable, or mission ready/combat mission ready) they are required to maintain.

Training Period—Any training period determined by the Wing in which training requirements are performed.

Upgrade Training—Training needed to qualify to a crew position of additional responsibility for a specific weapon system (e.g., special mission qualifications). See special mission event training.

Attachment 2

TRAINING PROGRESSION FLOW CHART

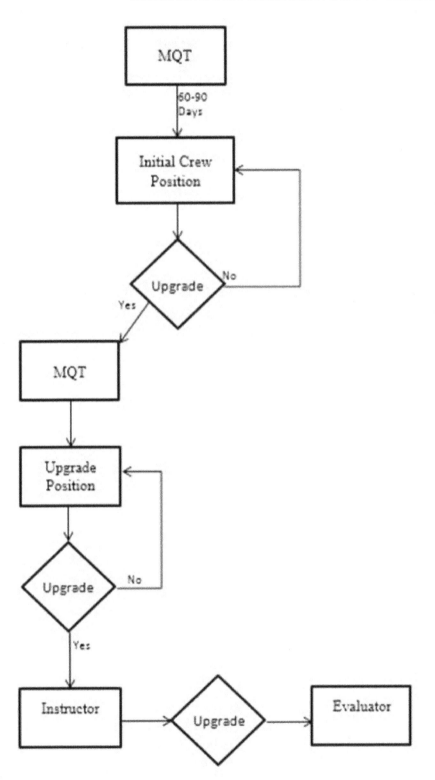

Attachment 3

CREW RESOURCE MANAGEMENT

Crew inventory requires close management at all levels to ensure a high state of readiness is maintained with available resources. To manage crew inventory, CPI codes are assigned to identify these positions.

Table A4.1. Crew Position Indicator Codes.

CPI Codes	Explanation	Remarks
1	Crew position used primarily for weapon system operations (Officer).	See Note 1
2	Crew position used primarily for weapon system operations (Government Civilians).	See Note 1
3	Staff or supervisory positions at wing level and below that have responsibilities and duties that require cyberspace operations expertise but which do not require the incumbents to operate the weapon system.	See Note 2
4	Staff or supervisory positions above the wing level that have responsibilities and duties that require cyberspace operations expertise but which do not require the incumbents to operate the weapon system.	See Note 2
6	Staff or supervisory positions at wing level and below that have responsibilities and duties that require the incumbents to actively perform cyberspace operational duties on the weapon system.	See Note 2
8	Staff or supervisory positions above the wing level that have responsibilities and duties that require the incumbent to actively conduct cyberspace operations on the weapon system.	See Note 2
A	Crew positions used primarily for weapon system operations (Enlisted).	See Note 1
B	Staff or supervisory positions at wing level and below that have responsibilities and duties that require the incumbents to actively perform cyberspace operational duties on the weapon system.	See Note 2
C	Staff or supervisory positions at wing level and below that have responsibilities and duties that require cyberspace operations expertise but which do not require the incumbents to actively operate the weapon system.	See Note 2
D	Staff or supervisory positions above the wing level that have responsibilities and duties that require the incumbent to actively conduct cyberspace operations on a weapon system.	See Note 2
E	Staff or supervisory positions above the wing level that have responsibilities and duties that require cyberspace operations expertise but which do not require the incumbents to actively operate the weapon system.	See Note 2

CPI Codes	Explanation	Remarks
Z	Crew positions used primarily for weapon system operations (Contractor).	See Note 1

Notes:

1. CPI-1, 2, A and Z are for officers, enlisted, government civilian, and contractor personnel assigned to operational squadrons or formal training programs. The primary duty of these personnel is to operate the weapon system to conduct cyberspace operations.

2. CPI-3, 4, 6, 8, B, C, D, and E identify crew members assigned to supervisory or staff positions. These positions require cyberspace operations experience with some requiring weapon system operation (CPI-6, 8, B, and D).

BY ORDER OF THE
SECRETARY OF THE AIR FORCE

AIR FORCE INSTRUCTION 17-2NAS
VOLUME 2

10 FEBRUARY 2017

Cyberspace

NETWORK ATTACK SYSTEM (NAS)
STANDARDIZATION AND
EVALUATION

COMPLIANCE WITH THIS PUBLICATION IS MANDATORY

ACCESSIBILITY: Publications and forms are available for downloading or ordering on the e-Publishing website at www.e-publishing.af.mil.

RELEASABILITY: There are no releaseability restrictions on this publication.

OPR: AF/A3CO/A6CO

Certified by: AF/A3C/A6C
(Brig Gen Kevin E. Kennedy)
Pages: 25

This instruction volume implements Air Force (AF) Policy Directive (AFPD) 17-2, Cyberspace Operations and Air Force Instruction (AFI) 17-202V2, *Cybercrew Standardization and Evaluation*. It establishes the Cybercrew Standardization and Evaluation (Stan/Eval) procedures and evaluation criteria for qualifying cybercrew members in the Network Attack System (NAS) weapon system. This publication applies to all military and civilian AF personnel, members of AF Reserve Command (AFRC) units and the Air National Guard (ANG). Refer to paragraph 1.3 for information on the authority to waive provisions of this AFI. This publication may be supplemented at the unit level, but all direct supplements must be routed through channels to HQ USAF/A6S for coordination prior to certification and approval. Lead Major Command (MAJCOM)-provided instructions may contain additional specific Stan/Eval requirements unique to individual and cybercrew positions. Send recommended changes or comments to the Office of Primary Responsibility (HQ USAF/A3CO/A6CO, 1480 Air Force Pentagon, Washington, DC 20330-1480), using AF Form 847, Recommendation for Change of Publication; route AF Forms 847 from the field through the chain of command. This instruction requires collecting and maintaining information protected by the Privacy Act of 1974 (5 U.S.C. 552a). System of records notices F036 AF PC C, Military Personnel Records System, and OPM/GOVT-1, General Personnel Records, apply. When collecting and maintaining information protect it by the Privacy Act of 1974 authorized by 10 U.S.C. 8013.

The authorities to waive wing/unit level requirements in this publication are identified with a Tier ("T-0, T-1, T-2, T-3") number following the compliance statement. See AFI 33-360,

AFI17-2NASV2 10 FEBRUARY 2017

Publications and Forms Management, Table 1.1 for descriptions of the authorities associated with the Tier numbers. Submit requests for waivers through the chain of command to the appropriate Tier waiver approval authority, or alternately, to the Publication Office of Primary Responsibility (OPR) for non-tiered compliance items. Refer recommended changes and questions about this publication to the OPR using the AF Form 847, Recommendation for Change of Publication; route AF Form 847s from the field through MAJCOM publications/forms managers to AF/A3C/A6C. Ensure all records created as a result of processes prescribed in this publication are maintained in accordance with AF Manual (AFMAN) 33-363, *Management of Records* and disposed of in accordance with the AF Records Disposition Schedule (RDS) located in the AF Records Management Information System (AFRIMS).

Chapter 1

GENERAL INFORMATION

1.1. General. This instruction provides cyberspace operations examiners and cybercrew members with procedures and evaluation criteria used during performance evaluations on operational cyberspace weapon systems. For evaluation purposes, refer to this AFI for evaluation standards. Adherence to these procedures and criteria will ensure an accurate assessment of the proficiency and capabilities of cybercrew members. In addition to general criteria information and grading criteria, this AFI provides specific information and grading criteria for each crew position, special mission qualification (SMQ), instructor upgrade qualification, and unit Standards and Evaluations Examiner (SEE) objectivity evaluations.

1.2. Recommendation for Change of Publication. Recommendations for improvements to this volume will be submitted on AF Form 847, *Recommendation for Change of Publication*, through the appropriate chain of command to HQ USAF/A3CO/A6CO. Approved recommendations will be collated into interim or formal change notices, and forwarded to HQ 24 AF/A3T for 24 AF/A3 approval.

1.3. Waivers. Route waiver requests through the Numbered Air Force (NAF) for comment. Waiver approval authority for cyberspace weapon-specific crew requirements is HQ AFSPC/A2/3/6T (ANG: NGB/A3), unless otherwise specified in this volume. HQ AFRC/A3T is the waiver authority for reserve units. AFSPC gained units process waivers IAW this paragraph. The reserve group commander submits waiver requests through 10 AF/A3 to HQ AFRC/A3T. HQ AFRC/A3T provides a copy of the waiver request and HQ AFRC/A3T waiver decision to HQ AFSPC/A2/3/6T. All waiver requests must include the following, as applicable:

1.3.1. Name, rank, crew position, type weapon system, type of evaluation, expiration date, and applicable paragraph.

1.3.2. Justification for waiver (submit specific, detailed justification).

1.3.3. Unit plan of action (submit specific, detailed plan of action).

1.4. Procedures.

1.4.1. SEEs will use the grading policies contained in AFI 17-202V2 and the evaluation criteria in this instruction for conducting all AFSPC and AFSPC-oversight units' weapon system performance and Emergency Procedures Evaluations (EPE). All evaluations assume a stable platform and normal operating conditions. **(T-3)**

1.4.2. Squadron will design and maintain evaluation profiles for each NAS CMR position. These profiles, approved by the Operations Group (OG) Stan/Eval office (OGV), should outline the minimum number and type of events to be performed/observed in order to satisfy a complete evaluation. Evaluation profiles will incorporate requirements set in the applicable grading criteria and reflect the primary unit tasking. **(T-3)**

1.4.3. All evaluations fall under the Qualification (QUAL), Mission (MSN) or Spot (SPOT) categories listed in AFI 17-202V2. For specific details on updating the AF Form 4418, refer to unit Operating Instructions. **(T-3)**

1.4.3.1. Schedule all evaluation activity on one sortie to the greatest extent possible. All performance phase requirements should be accomplished during a simulated sortie. **(T-3)**

1.4.3.2. During all evaluations, any events observed by the evaluator may be evaluated. If additional training is required for areas outside of the scheduled evaluation, document the training required under the appropriate area on the AF Form 4418. **(T-3)**

1.4.3.3. Written requisites and the grading criteria for various evaluations can be found at a higher classification. For copies of this material, requestors must contact the unit Security Office.

1.4.3.4. Unit examiners may give evaluations outside of their organization to include administering evaluations between AFSPC, AFRC and ANG provided written agreements/understandings between the affected organizations are in-place. Written agreements/understandings shall be reviewed and updated annually. **(T-2)**

1.4.4. Momentary deviations from tolerances will not be considered in the grading, provided the examinee applies prompt corrective action and such deviations do not jeopardize safety or the mission. Cumulative deviations will be considered when determining the overall grade. The SEE will state the examinee's overall rating, review with the examinee the area grades assigned, thoroughly critique specific deviations, and recommend/assign any required additional training. **(T-3)**

1.4.5. Use evaluators as instructors for any phase of training for which they are qualified to capitalize on their expertise and experience. SEEs will not evaluate students with whom they have instructed 50% of the qualification/upgrade training or those they recommend for qualification/upgrade evaluation without Squadron (SQ)/CC approval. Additionally, SEEs will not evaluate direct supervisors or personal on their assigned crew without SQ/CC approval. **(T-3)**

1.4.6. All crewmembers for the mission/sortie (to include students, instructors, examinees, and evaluators) will participate in and adhere to all required mission planning, mission briefing, mission execution, and mission debriefing requirements. **(T-3)**

1.5. General Evaluation Requirements.

1.5.1. Publications Check. The squadron Mission Management office will list all required publications for employment of the NAS. **(T-3)**

1.5.2. Written Examinations:

1.5.2.1. The written examination will be accomplished prior to the mission/sortie performance phase unless in conjunction with a No-Notice (N/N) QUAL. **(T-3)**

1.5.3. Emergency Action Procedures (EAP). Every Qualification evaluation which updates an expiration date will include an EAP. EAPs will evaluate the crewmember's knowledge and/or performance of emergency procedures, to include use of emergency equipment. **(T-3)**

1.5.4. Qualification (QUAL) Evaluations. These evaluations measure a crewmember's ability to meet grading areas listed in unit Operating Instructions in accordance with (IAW) AFI 17-202V2 and weapon system-specific guidance. When practical, QUAL evaluations should be combined with Instructor evaluations, as applicable for the crew position. **(T-3)**

1.5.5. Mission (MSN) Evaluations. IAW AFI 17-202V2 and weapon system-specific guidance, the requirement for a separate MSN evaluation may be combined with the QUAL evaluation. Mission certifications will be IAW AFI 17-202 Vol 1, AFI 17-2.NAS Vol 1, and all applicable supplements and will be documented in the appropriate training folder. **(T-3)**

1.5.5.1. For cybercrew members who maintain multiple mission certifications, recurring evaluations need only evaluate the primary mission events as long as currency is maintained in all other required training events. **(T-3)**

1.5.6. Instructor Evaluations. Grading areas for these evaluations are listed in unit Operating Instructions and must meet all requirements from AFI 17-202V2 and weapon system-specific guidance. **(T-3)**

1.5.7. SEE Objectivity Evaluations. Grading areas for these evaluations are listed in unit Operating Instructions and must meet all requirements from AFI 17-202V2 and weapon system-specific guidance. **(T-3)**

1.5.8. No-Notice Evaluations. The Operations Group Commander (OG/CC) will determine no-notice evaluation procedures/goals. **(T-3)**

1.6. Grading Instructions. Standards and performance parameters are contained in AFI 17-202V2 and this instruction. A three-level grading system is used for most areas; however a "Q-" grade will not be indicated under critical areas. **(T-3)**

1.6.1. Critical Area/Subarea. Critical areas are events that require adequate accomplishment by the examinee in order to successfully and safely achieve the mission/sortie objectives and complete the evaluation. These events, if not adequately accomplished could result in mission failure, endanger human life, or cause serious injury or death. Additionally, critical areas/subareas apply to time-sensitive tasks or tasks that must be accomplished as expeditiously as possible without any intervening lower priority actions that would, in the normal sequence of events, adversely affect task performance/outcome. If an examinee receives a "U" grade in any critical area, the overall grade for the evaluation will be "Q-3." Critical areas are identified by "(C)" following the applicable area title. **(T-3)**

1.6.2. Major Area/Subarea. Major areas are events or tasks deemed integral to the performance of other tasks and required to sustain acceptable weapon system operations and mission execution. If an examinee receives a "U" grade in a non-critical area then the overall grade awarded will be no higher than "Q-2." An examinee receiving a "Q-" grade in a non-critical area or areas may still receive a "Q-1" overall grade at evaluator discretion. An overall "Q-3" can be awarded if, in the judgment of the SEE, there is justification based on performance in one or several areas/sub areas. Major areas are identified by "(M)" following the applicable area title. **(T-3)**

1.6.3. Minor Area/Subarea. Minor areas are rudimentary or simple tasks related to weapons system operations that by themselves have little or no impact on mission execution. Minor areas are identified by "(m)" following the applicable area title. **(T-3)**

1.6.4. If an examinee receives a "U" grade in a non-critical (major or minor) area then the overall grade awarded will be no higher than "Q-2." An examinee receiving a "Q-" grade in a non-critical area or areas may still receive a "Q-1" overall grade at evaluator discretion. An overall "Q-3" can be awarded if, in the judgment of the SEE, there is justification based on performance in one or several areas/sub areas. **(T-3)**

1.6.5. The SEE must exercise judgment when the wording of areas is subjective and when specific situations are not covered. **(T-3)**

1.6.6. Evaluator judgment will be the final determining factor in deciding the overall qualification level. **(T-3)**

Table 1.1. Crew Position/Upgrade Evaluation Requirements (T-3).

AREA/TITLE	Category C, M, m	Crew Position				Upgrade	
		CC	OC	CO	OT	INSTR	SEE OBJ
1. Mission Planning	M	R	R	R	R		
2. Briefing	M	R	R	R	R		
3. Positional Changeover	M, Note 1	R	R	R	R		
4. Safety	C	R	R	R	R		
5. Emergency Equipment / Procedures	M	R	R	R	R		
6. Crew Discipline	C	R	R	R	R		
7. Situational Awareness	C	R	R	R	R		
8. Mission Checks/Checklist Procedures	M	R	R	R	R		
9. Crew Coordination	M	R	R	R	R		
10. Task Management	M	R	R	R	R		
11. Employment Timing	M	R	R	R			
12. System Knowledge Operations	M	R	R	R	R		
13. Communication	M	R	R	R	R		
14. Reports/Logs/Forms	M	R	R	R	R		
15. Post Mission Activity	M	R	R	R	R		
16. Debrief	M	R	R	R	R		
17. Mission Management	M	R	R				
18. Dynamic/Time Sensitive Target	M	R	R				
Instructor Upgrade Evaluation Criteria							
19. Instructional Ability	M					R	
20. Instructional Briefings / Critique	M					R	
21. Demonstration and Performance	M					R	
Stan/Eval Examiner Objectivity Evaluation Criteria							
22. Compliance with Stan/Eval Directives	M						R
23. Stan/Eval Examiner (SEE) Briefing	M						R
24. Performance Assessment and Grading	M						R
25. Assessment of Overall Performance	M						R
26. Assignment of Additional Training	M, Note 2						R
27. Mission Critique	M						R

C – critical; M – major; m – minor
R – required
NOTES:
1. Applicable for shift/crew changeovers.
2. If required by examinee's performance.

Chapter 2

CREW POSITION EVALUATIONS AND GRADING CRITERIA

2.1. General. The grading criteria contained in this chapter apply to evaluations for NAS crew commanders, operations controllers, operators, and technicians. These criteria were derived from experience, policies, and procedures set forth in weapon system manuals and other directives. Evaluators must realize that grading criteria contained herein cannot accommodate every situation. Written parameters must be tempered with mission objectives and, more importantly, mission/task accomplishment in the determination of overall aircrew performance. Requirements for each evaluation are as follows:

2.2. Qualification Evaluations.

   2.2.1. Written Examination Requisites will be detailed in unit Operating Instructions. **(T-3)**

   2.2.2. Emergency Procedures Evaluations will be detailed in unit Operating Instructions. **(T-3)**

   2.2.3. Performance Phase: The SEE will follow a pre-planned script/scenario to evaluate a member and ensure standardization and consistency of the Evaluation Process. **(T-2)** Details of the process can be found in the unit Operating Instructions and in unit Stan/Eval materials at a higher classification. **(T-3)**

2.3. Mission Certifications. Mission Certifications ensure that individuals are capable of performing duties essential to the effective employment of the weapon system. Mission Certifications are accomplished IAW local training requirements and/or SQ/CC directions. **(T-3)**

2.4. General Crew Position Evaluation Criteria. The following general evaluation grading criteria are common to all crew positions and will be used for all applicable evaluations: **(T-3)**

   2.4.1. AREA 1, Mission Planning (M).

      2.4.1.1. Q. Led or contributed to mission planning efforts IAW procedures prescribed in applicable guidance manuals, instructions, and directives. Planning adequately addressed mission objectives and/or tasking. Plan adequately considered intelligence information, weapon system capability/operating status, and crew composition/ability with minor errors/deviations/missions that did not impact mission effectiveness. Verified review of all Cybercrew Information File (CIF) Vol 1, Part B items and complied with Go/No-Go procedures prior to mission start. Was prepared at briefing time. **(T-3)**

      2.4.1.2. Q-. Errors/deviations/omissions had minor impact on mission effectiveness or efficiencies, but did not impact mission accomplishment or jeopardize mission success. **(T-3)**

      2.4.1.3. U. Failed to adequately lead mission planning effort. Failed to review CIF and/or comply with Go/No-Go procedures. Failures to comply with procedures prescribed in applicable guidance manuals, instructions, and directives contributed to significant deficiencies in mission execution / accomplishment. Failed to lead or participate in all required briefings and/or planning meetings without appropriate approval. **(T-3)**

2.4.2. AREA 2, Briefing (M).

2.4.2.1. Q. Led or contributed to briefing effort as appropriate. Well organized and presented in a logical sequence, appropriate timeframe, and professional manner. Effectively incorporated briefing/training aids and presented all training events and effective techniques required for accomplishing the mission. [NOTE - Upgrade positions must also include: .Briefed CIFs and crew Go/No-Go status.] Crewmembers clearly understood roles, responsibilities, and mission requirements. Minor errors/omissions/deviations did not impact mission effectiveness or efficiencies. **(T-3)**

2.4.2.2. Q-. Led or contributed to briefing effort with minor errors/omissions/deviations. Some events out of sequence with some unnecessary redundancy. Briefing anomalies had minor impact on mission effectiveness but did not jeopardize mission success. **(T-3)**

2.4.2.3. U. Inadequate leadership or participation in briefing development and/or presentation. Disorganized and/or confusing presentation. Ineffective use of briefing/training aids. [NOTE - Upgrade positions must also include: Failed to brief required topics/discussion areas prescribed in directives. Failed to present major training events. Failed to brief required and crew Go/No-Go status.] Errors/omissions/deviations impacted crew ability to accomplish the mission. Absent from briefing (whole or in-part) without appropriate supervisor approval. **(T-3)**

2.4.3. AREA 3, Positional Changeover Brief (M).

2.4.3.1. Q. Outgoing crewmember prepared and conducted a comprehensive positional changeover briefing with the oncoming crewmember IAW checklist(s) and applicable directives. Reviewed factors, conditions, and the current operational/tactical situation for all executing packages, sorties, etc. with the oncoming crew member and ensured items necessary for the effective conduct of tasked missions were understood by the oncoming crewmember. Minor errors/omissions/deviations did not impact mission effectiveness. Oncoming crewmember was attentive and asked questions as applicable to ensure mission effectiveness/accomplishment. **(T-3)**

2.4.3.2. Q-. Outgoing crewmember prepared and conducted a positional changeover briefing with minor errors/omissions/deviations using checklist(s) and applicable directives. Changeover briefing anomalies had minor impact on mission effectiveness but did not jeopardize mission success. Oncoming crew member's level of attentiveness during changeover led to minor mission impact but did not jeopardize overall mission success. **(T-3)**

2.4.3.3. U. Outgoing crewmember failed to prepare and conduct an effective positional changeover briefing with the oncoming crewmember and/or failed to use appropriate checklist(s) and applicable directives. Changeover briefing contained errors/omissions/deviations that could have significantly detracted from mission effectiveness and/or jeopardized mission success. Oncoming crew member's lack of attentiveness and/or inadequate requests for clarification could have significantly detracted from mission effectiveness and/or jeopardized mission success. **(T-3)**

2.4.4. AREA 4, Safety (C).

2.4.4.1. Q. Aware of and complied with all factors required for safe operations and mission accomplishment. **(T-3)**

2.4.4.2. U. Was not aware of safety factors or disregarded procedures to safely operate and conduct the mission. Conducted unsafe actions that jeopardized mission accomplishment and/or put crewmembers at risk of injury or death. Operated in a manner that could or did result in damage to the weapon system/equipment. **(T-3)**

2.4.5. AREA 5, Emergency Procedures and Equipment (M).

2.4.5.1. Q. Recognized emergency situations or malfunctions and immediately demonstrated /explained appropriate response actions. Demonstrated/explained thorough knowledge of location and proper use of emergency equipment. Demonstrated/explained effective coordinated emergency actions with other crewmembers without delay or confusion. Followed appropriate checklists as required. [NOTE: Crew Commander is responsible for inspecting/verifying the required contents of the flyaway kit.] Minor errors did not impact efficiencies in addressing the emergency. (This area may be evaluated orally.) **(T-3)**

2.4.5.2. Q-. Recognized emergency situations or malfunctions but slow to demonstrate/explain appropriate response actions. Examinee demonstrated/explained correct procedures with minor errors and/or was slow to locate equipment and/or appropriate checklists. Slow or hesitant to demonstrate/explain coordinated emergency actions with other crewmembers. Minor checklist errors/omissions/deviations caused minor inefficiencies addressing the emergency situation/malfunction but did not exacerbate the situation. **(T-3)**

2.4.5.3. U. Failed to recognize emergency situations or malfunctions. Failed to demonstrate/explain proper response actions. Failed to demonstrate /explain knowledge of location or proper use of emergency equipment or checklists. Failed to demonstrate/explain coordinated emergency actions with other crewmembers. Checklist errors/omissions/deviations contributed to ineffective actions or exacerbating an emergency situation and/or malfunction. **(T-3)**

2.4.6. AREA 6, Crew Discipline (C).

2.4.6.1. Q. Demonstrated strict professional crew discipline throughout all phases of the mission. Led or supported (based on crew position) the planning, briefing, execution, and debriefing of the mission in accordance with applicable instructions and directives. **(T-3)**

2.4.6.2. U. Failed to demonstrate strict professional crew discipline throughout all phases of the mission. Violated or failed to comply with applicable instructions and directives which could have jeopardized safety of crewmembers or mission accomplishment. **(T-3)**

2.4.7. AREA 7, Airmanship / Situational Awareness (C).

2.4.7.1. Q. Conducted the mission with a sense of understanding/comprehension and in a timely, efficient manner. Anticipated situations which would have adversely affected the mission and made appropriate decisions based on available information. Maintained overall good situational awareness. Recognized temporary loss of situational awareness in self or others and took appropriate action to regain awareness without detracting from mission accomplishment or jeopardizing safety. **(T-3)**

2.4.7.2. U. Decisions or lack thereof resulted in failure to accomplish the assigned mission. Demonstrated poor judgment or lost situational awareness to the extent that safety and/or mission accomplishment could have been compromised. **(T-3)**

2.4.8. AREA 8, Mission Checks / Checklist Procedures (M).

2.4.8.1. Q. Performed all mission/operations checks as required. Efficient location and proficient/timely accomplishment checklists. Adequately ensured, determined, and/or verified weapon system operational state and cybercrew readiness prior to on-watch period or entering tasked vulnerability period. Ensured crew understanding of most up-to-date tasking(s) prior to on-watch or vulnerability period execution. Deviated from checklists and/or omitted steps only when appropriate and was able to substantiate justification. Minor errors/deviations/omissions did not detract from mission efficiencies nor jeopardize mission success. **(T-3)**

2.4.8.2. Q-. Same as qualified, except minor errors/deviations/omissions detracted from mission efficiencies but did not jeopardize overall mission success. **(T-3)**

2.4.8.3. U. Did not perform mission/operations checks or monitor systems to the degree that an emergency /unsafe condition would have developed or damage to equipment would have occurred if allowed to continue uncorrected. Failed to determine/verify weapon system operational state and cybercrew readiness prior to on-watch period or entering tasked vulnerability period. Unable to locate the appropriate checklist, used incorrect checklist, or consistently omitted checklist items without substantiated justification. Excessive delay in completing required checklist. Errors/deviations/omissions contributed to jeopardizing mission success. **(T-3)**

2.4.9. AREA 9, Crew Coordination (M).

2.4.9.1. Q. Effectively coordinated with other crewmembers during all phases of the mission enabling efficient, well-coordinated actions. Demonstrated basic knowledge of other crewmembers' duties and responsibilities. Proactively provided direction and/or information to the crew; communicated in a clear and effective manner, actively sought other crewmember opinions and/or ideas, and asked for or gave constructive feedback as necessary. **(T-3)**

2.4.9.2. Q-. Some breakdowns in communication but did not detract from overall mission success. Limited in basic knowledge of other crewmembers' duties/responsibilities. Unclear communication at times caused confusion and/or limited crew interaction. Some unnecessary prompting required from other crewmembers. **(T-3)**

2.4.9.3. U. Severe breakdowns in coordination precluded possible mission ineffectiveness/failure or jeopardized safety of crewmembers. Lacked basic knowledge of other crewmember's duties and responsibilities. Unclear/lack of communication or excessive prompting required by crewmembers put mission and/or safety of others at risk. **(T-3)**

2.4.10. AREA 10, Task Management (M).

2.4.10.1. Q. Assured mission success by correctly identifying, prioritizing, and managing tasks based on existing and new information. Used available resources to manage workload and requested assistance when required. Effectively identified contingencies and solutions. Minor errors/omissions but did not result in inefficiencies nor jeopardize mission success. **(T-3)**

2.4.10.2. Q-. Minor omissions and/or errors (which did not affect safety of crewmembers) led to mission inefficiencies but did not jeopardize mission accomplishment. Limited use of available resources to aid decision making, manage workload, and/or slow to request assistance from other crew members when needed. **(T-3)**

2.4.10.3. U. Failed to identify, prioritize, or manage tasks leading to possible unsafe conditions or significant risk to mission accomplishment. Inability to identify contingencies, ineffective decision making, or errors/omissions placed mission accomplishment and/or safety of others at risk. **(T-3)**

2.4.11. AREA 11, Employment Timing (M).

2.4.11.1. Q. Effectively met mission timings and accomplished 80% or greater of all tasking within assigned TOT window. **(T-3)**

2.4.11.2. Q-. Minor errors but effectively met most mission timings; accomplished at least 60% to 80% of tasking within assigned TOT. **(T-3)**

2.4.11.3. U. Unable to meet critical mission timing requirements resulting in severe degradation or failure of the mission. Failed to meet Q- requirements for meeting TOT and tasking accomplishment threshold. **(T-3)**

2.4.12. AREA 12, Systems Knowledge / Operations (M).

2.4.12.1. Q. Demonstrated thorough knowledge of weapon system components (i.e. equipment, console, applications, tools, and/or software), performance characteristics, employment, and operating procedures. Employed appropriate tactics, techniques, and procedures (TTPs) and made adjustments as necessary throughout all phases of the mission. Correctly identified and applied proper action(s) for system component equipment malfunctions. Followed all applicable system component operating directives, guides, manuals, checklists etc. **(T-3)**

2.4.12.2. Q-. Minor deficiencies or errors resulted in inefficiencies but performance was sufficient to accomplish the mission safely. Did not damage system/components/equipment. **(T-3)**

2.4.12.3. U. Demonstrated severe lack of knowledge of weapon system components/equipment, limitations, performance characteristics, employment or operating procedures. Unable to adequately apply TTPs to accomplish the mission. Failed to identify malfunctions and/or apply corrective actions. Failed to follow system/equipment operating directives, guides, manuals, etc resulting in unsatisfactory employment. Poor procedures/errors resulted in damage to system components/equipment or jeopardized mission failure. **(T-3)**

2.4.13. AREA 13, Communication (M).

2.4.13.1. Q. Timely and effective communication with external agencies and/or mission partners when required. Concise and accurate information passed using proper medium, terminology, format and/or brevity. Sound understanding and use of crew position-relevant voice, email, chat, and collaborative tools to communicate mission essential information. Demonstrated a thorough understanding of Communications Security (COMSEC)/Operational Security (OPSEC) procedures. **(T-3)**

2.4.13.2. Q-. Minor errors/deviations/omissions in communications with external agencies and/or mission partners that did not detract from overall mission accomplishment. Limited understanding and use of crew position-relevant voice, email, chat, and collaborative tools. Demonstrated limited understanding of COMSEC/OPSEC procedures with minor errors or deviations that did not jeopardize mission accomplishment. **(T-3)**

2.4.13.3. U. Severe breakdowns in communication with external agencies and/or mission partners precluded possible mission ineffectiveness/failure or jeopardized safety of others. Unclear/inaccurate information passed or improper/inadequate use of medium, terminology, format, and/or brevity put mission accomplishment at risk. Significant COMSEC/OPSEC errors or deviations jeopardized mission accomplishment. **(T-3)**

2.4.14. AREA 14, Reports/Logs/Forms (M) (This area may be evaluated orally.)

2.4.14.1. Q. Recognized all situations meeting reporting criteria. When required, provided timely, accurate, and correctly formatted reports [e.g. Mission Summary (MISUM)] or inputs to mission-related information management portals/collaborative information sharing environments. All required logs [i.e. Master Station Log (MSL)], media and forms were complete, accurate, legible, and accomplished on time and IAW with applicable directives, tasking, and policy. Information was provided in sufficient detail to allow accurate and timely analysis of associated data. Complied with security procedures and directives. **(T-3)**

2.4.14.2. Q-. Minor errors/ deviations/omissions/latency on required reports, logs, media, or forms led to minor inefficiencies but did not affect conduct of the mission. Complied with security procedures and directives. **(T-3)**

2.4.14.3. U. Failed to recognize situations meeting reporting criteria and/or failure to report events essential to mission accomplishment. Major errors/deviations/omissions/latency in accomplishing logs, reports/inputs, media, or forms precluded effective mission accomplishment or analysis of mission data. Failed to comply with security procedures and directives. **(T-3)**

2.4.15. AREA 15, Post Mission Activity (M).

2.4.15.1. Q. Accomplished and/or supervised timely post-mission checks, system shutdown procedures, and workstation clean up IAW applicable checklists, guidance, and directives. **(T-3)**

2.4.15.2. Q-. Minor deviations, omissions, or errors but did not adversely impact mission effectiveness, cause damage to systems/equipment, or risk safety of others. **(T-3)**

2.4.15.3. U. Major deviations, omissions, and/or errors were made in performance of post-mission procedures, which could have jeopardized mission effectiveness, caused equipment damage, or endangered others. **(T-3)**

2.4.16. AREA 16, Debrief (M).

2.4.16.1. Q. Thoroughly debriefed the mission and/or contributed to the briefing content to ensure it included all pertinent items. [Note – Evaluated for upgrade positions only: Reconstructed operational events, compared results with initial objectives for the mission, debriefed deviations, and provided individual crew member feedback as appropriate. Organized IAW guidance/directives and professionally presented in a logical sequence using available briefing aids. Summarized lessons learned and ensured they were documented.] Provided crew commander/operations controller with applicable input on all required mission/crew/system-related events, including mission log/report/database information for inclusion in the crew debrief. Used applicable checklist(s) as required. Minor errors/omissions/deviations did not impact mission effectiveness or efficiencies. **(T-3)**

2.4.16.2. Q-. Led or contributed to debriefing effort with minor errors/omissions/deviations. Some events out of sequence with some unnecessary redundancy. Briefing or input anomalies had minor impact on mission effectiveness but did not jeopardize mission success. **(T-3)**

2.4.16.3. U. Inadequate leadership or participation in briefing development and/or presentation. [Note – Evaluated for upgrade positions only: Disorganized and/or confusing presentation. Ineffective use of briefing/training aids. Failed to reconstruct operational events, compare results with initial objectives for the mission, debrief deviations, and/or offer corrective guidance as appropriate.] Absent from briefing (whole or in-part) without appropriate supervisor approval. Errors, omissions, or deviations jeopardized mission success. **(T-3)**

2.5. Crew Commander / Operations Controller Specific Evaluation Criteria. The following evaluation grading criteria are common to the Crew Commander and Operations Controller crew positions and will be used for all applicable evaluations:

2.5.1. AREA 17, Mission Management (M).

2.5.1.1. Q. Assured mission success by accurately identifying, effectively prioritizing, and efficiently managing mission tasks based on planned and updated information. Identified contingencies, gathered data, and formulated decisions. Clearly communicated task priorities and updates to crew members. Used available resources necessary to manage workload, monitor crew activity, and aid in decision making. **(T-3)**

2.5.1.2. Q-. Minor omissions and/or errors which did not affect safety of crewmembers or effective mission accomplishment. Limited use of available resources to aid decision making, manage workload, and/or communicate task priorities/updates to other crew members. **(T-3)**

2.5.1.3. U. Failed to identify, prioritize, or manage mission tasks leading to possible unsafe conditions or significant risk to mission accomplishment. Improperly or unable to identify contingencies, gather data, or communicate decisions putting mission accomplishment and/or safety of others at risk. Failed to communicate task priorities/updates to crew members or adequately monitor crew activity. **(T-3)**

2.5.2. AREA 18, Dynamic/Time Sensitive Targeting (M).

2.5.2.1. Q. Effective coordination with outside agencies and timely contract execution resulted in prompt employment/engagement IAW the ROE, given restrictions or tactical situation. **(T-3)**

2.5.2.2. Q-. Although remaining IAW ROE, minor errors caused delayed contract execution or less than optimal coordination with outside agencies resulted in delayed employment/engagement. **(T-3)**

2.5.2.3. U. Major errors delayed or prevented contract execution and/or resulted in employment/engagement failure. Employment/engagement was outside the ROE, given restrictions, or tactical situation. **(T-3)**

Chapter 3

INSTRUCTOR EVALUATIONS AND GRADING CRITERIA

3.1. General. Grading criteria contained herein cannot accommodate every situation. Written parameters must be tempered with sortie objectives, evaluator judgment, and task accomplishment in the determination of overall crew performance. **(T-3)**

3.2. Instructor Upgrade and Qualification Requisites. Prior to an initial Instructor Evaluation, Instructor examinees must have completed all requisites for Instructor upgrade consideration, nomination and training IAW AFI 17-202 Vol 1, AFI 17-2.NAS Vol 1, and all applicable supplemental guidance. **(T-3)**

3.3. Instructor Qualification Evaluations. When possible, units should strive to combine instructor evaluations (initial and recurring/periodic) with periodic QUAL evaluations. Instructor evaluations can only be combined with QUAL evaluations when the examinee is in their periodic QUAL eligibility period. **(T-3)**

3.3.1. Initial Instructor evaluations should be conducted with a student occupying the applicable cybercrew position whenever possible. Recurring or periodic Instructor Evaluations may be conducted with the SEE role playing as the student. **(T-3)**

3.3.2. The instructor examinee will monitor all phases of the mission from an advantageous position and be prepared to demonstrate or explain any area or procedure. The SEE will particularly note the instructor's ability to recognize student difficulties and provide effective, timely instruction and/or corrective action. The SEE should also evaluate the grade assigned and the completed grade sheet or event training form for the student on all initial instructor checks. **(T-3)**

3.3.3. The student will perform those duties prescribed by the instructor for the mission/sortie being accomplished. If an actual student is not available, the SEE will identify to the examinee (prior to the mission) the level of performance to be expected from the SEE acting as the student. If this option is utilized, at least one event or briefing must be instructed. **(T-3)**

3.3.4. Periodic instructor evaluations will be administered in conjunction with required periodic qualification evaluations. (T-3) The examinee must occupy the primary duty position for an adequate period of time to demonstrate proficiency in the crew position with required qualification evaluations. All instructor evaluations will include a pre-mission and post-mission briefing. **(T-3)**

3.3.5. Awarding a "U" in any of the Instructor Grading Criteria areas will result in a Q-3 for the overall instructor grade. The overall grade for the instructor portion of the evaluation will be no higher than the lowest overall grade awarded under QUAL. **(T-3)**

3.3.6. Instructor Evaluation Grading Criteria. All Instructor Evaluation Criteria must be observed and graded to ensure a complete evaluation. The following general evaluation grading criteria are common to all crew positions and will be used for all applicable instructor evaluations: (T-3)

3.3.7. AREA 19, Instructional Ability (M).

3.3.7.1. Q. Demonstrated ability to communicate effectively. Provided appropriate corrective guidance when necessary. Planned ahead and made timely decisions. Correctly analyzed student errors. **(T-3)**

3.3.7.2. Q-. Minor discrepancies in the above criteria that did not adversely impact student progress. **(T-3)**

3.3.7.3. U. Unable to effectively communicate with the student. Did not provide corrective action where necessary. Did not plan ahead or anticipate student problems. Incorrectly analyzed student errors. Adversely impacted student progress. **(T-3)**

3.3.8. AREA 20, Instructional Briefings/Critique (M).

3.3.8.1. Q. Briefings were well organized, accurate, and thorough. Reviewed student's present level of training and defined mission events to be performed. Demonstrated ability during critique to reconstruct the mission/sortie, offer mission analysis, and provide corrective guidance where appropriate. Completed all training documents according to prescribed directives. Appropriate grades awarded. **(T-3)**

3.3.8.2. Q-. As above but with minor errors or omissions in briefings, critique, or training documents that did not adversely impact student progress. **(T-3)**

3.3.8.3. U. Pre-mission or post-mission briefings were marginal or nonexistent. Did not review student's training folder or past performance. Failed to adequately critique student or conducted an incomplete mission analysis which compromised learning. Student strengths or weaknesses were not identified. Adversely impacted student progress. Inappropriate grades awarded. Overlooked or omitted major discrepancies. **(T-3)**

3.3.9. AREA 21, Demonstration and Performance (M).

3.3.9.1. Q. Effectively demonstrated procedures and techniques. Demonstrated thorough knowledge of weapon system/components, procedures, and all applicable publications and regulations. **(T-3)**

3.3.9.2. Q-. Minor discrepancies in the above criteria that did not adversely impact student progress. **(T-3)**

3.3.9.3. U. Did not demonstrate correct procedure or technique. Insufficient depth of knowledge about weapon system/components, procedures, or proper source material. Adversely impacted student progress. **(T-3)**

3.4. Instructor Evaluation Documentation.

3.4.1. Instructor Qualification Evaluations will be documented as a SPOT evaluation on the AF Form 4418 and AF Form 4420 and maintained in the member's cyber crew qualification folder IAW AFI 17-202 Vol 2, applicable higher headquarters supplements, and local supplemental guidance. **(T-3)** Additional Instructor Evaluation documentation is as follows:

3.4.2. Letter of Certifications.

3.4.2.1. Upon the successful completion of an Instructor Qualification Evaluation, units will ensure the crewmembers instructor status is reflected on the Letter of Certifications. **(T-3)**

3.4.2.2. Upon the expiration of a qualification or failure of an Instructor Qualification Evaluation, units will ensure the crewmembers instructor status is reflected on the Letter of Certifications. **(T-3)**

Chapter 4

SEE OBJECTIVITY EVALUATIONS AND GRADING CRITERIA

4.1. General. SEE Objectivity Evaluations are a vehicle for commanders to upgrade crewmembers for SEE qualification and a tool to monitor the evaluator crew force's adherence to Stan/Eval directives. Grading criteria contained herein cannot accommodate every situation. Written parameters must be tempered with sortie objectives, evaluator judgment, and task accomplishment in the determination of overall examinee performance. The criteria contained in this chapter are established by experience, policies, and procedures set forth in weapon system manuals and other directives. The criteria contained in this chapter are applicable to all SEE Objectivity Evaluations for NAS crewmembers. **(T-3)**

4.2. Evaluator Upgrade and Qualification Requisites. Evaluators will be chosen from the instructor pool of cybercrew members, thus being certified and selected from the most highly qualified and highly experienced cybercrew members. Training, certification, and decertification requirements for MR/CMR evaluators will be determined by OG/CCs. **(T-3)**

4.2.1. Wing/Group/Squadron. SEE Upgrade candidate nominations will be approved by the OG/CC in writing. Once approved, candidates must complete all SEE training IAW AFI 17-202 Vol 2, this instruction, and all applicable supplemental guidance. As a minimum, SEE training will consist of: **(T-3)**

4.2.1.1. Local SEE academics/instruction covering all Stan/Eval programs and procedures. Training completion should be documented on a locally developed OG/CC checklist along with a signed certificate from the OG/CC or OG/CD. Both checklist and certificate will be maintained in the unit Stan/Eval office. **(T-3)**

4.2.1.2. The candidate observing one entire evaluation performed by a qualified SEE. NOTE: To the maximum extent possible, SEE Upgrade candidates should observe evaluations conducted within the weapon system for which they are qualified, however when not practical, the observed evaluation may be conducted with a qualified SEE within in the same Group regardless of weapon system or crew position. Training completion should be documented on a locally developed OG/CC checklist and maintained in the unit Stan/Eval office. **(T-3)**

4.2.1.3. Completion of a SEE Objectivity Evaluation under the supervision of a qualified SEE. NOTE: The SEE Objectivity will be conducted within the weapon system and crew position for which the SEE Upgrade candidate (SEE Examinee) maintains qualification. See paragraph 4.5 for SEE Objectivity Evaluation (AF Form 4418) documentation guidance. **(T-3)**

4.3. SEE Objectivity Evaluations. There is no eligibility period or expiration date associated with a SEE Objectivity Evaluation. Once obtained, crewmembers maintain SEE qualification unless they fail a QUAL evaluation, fail an Instructor evaluation, fail a SEE Objectivity Evaluation, their weapon system QUAL expires, or upon their SEE appointment being revoked/rescinded by the appointing official. See paragraph 4.5. for SEE Objectivity Evaluation documentation guidance. **(T-3)**

4.3.1. Only a qualified cyberspace weapon system SEE may administer a SEE Objectivity Evaluation to a cyberspace SEE examinee. SEE Objectivity Evaluations may be administered by SEE Examiners that are qualified in a different cyberspace weapon system type or crew position from the SEE examinee. **(T-3)** NOTE. This is common when the SEE Objectivity Evaluation is in conjunction with a higher headquarters inspection.

4.3.2. SEE Objectivity Evaluations will ensure the SEE examinee (for example in the case of a SEE Objectivity Evaluation conducted as part of a higher headquarters inspection) observes and grades the entire mission activity of the QUAL examinee. Mission activity is defined as all mission planning, briefing, execution, and debrief activities for the mission/sortie. **(T-3)**

4.3.3. The SEE Upgrade candidate or SEE Examinee will brief the qualified SEE Examiner on all observations, grades, commendable/discrepancies (if any), recommended additional training, and other mission related debrief topics prior to debriefing the QUAL examinee and/or examinee's supervisor. **(T-3)**

4.3.4. The SEE Upgrade candidate or SEE Examinee will complete the AF Form 4418 and have the SEE Examiner review it for completeness and accuracy. The SEE Examiner's signature block and signature (not signature/block of the SEE Upgrade candidate or SEE Examinee) will be entered on the AF Form 4418. **(T-3)**

4.4. SEE Objectivity Evaluation Grading Criteria. All SEE Objectivity Evaluation Criteria must be observed and graded to ensure a complete evaluation. The following grading criteria will be used by SEE's when conducting SEE Objectivity Evaluations. (T-3) A grade of Q- requiring additional training or a grade of U in any area for the SEE Objectivity Examinee will require an overall rating of "3". Cumulative deviations will be considered when determining the overall rating of either "1" or "3". Specific requirements for each evaluation are as follows:

4.4.1. AREA 22, Compliance with Stan/Eval Directives (M).

4.4.1.1. Q. Complied with all directives pertaining to the administration of the evaluation. **(T-3)**

4.4.1.2. Q-. Complied with most directives. Deviations did not jeopardize the effectiveness of the evaluation or mission success/safety. **(T-3)**

4.4.1.3. U. Failed to comply with directives or allowed mission success/safety to be jeopardized. **(T-3)**

4.4.2. AREA 23, Stan/Eval Examiner (SEE) Briefing (M).

4.4.2.1. Q. Thoroughly briefed the examinee on the conduct of the evaluation, mission requirements, responsibilities, grading criteria, and examiner actions/position during the evaluation. **(T-3)**

4.4.2.2. Q-. Items were omitted during the briefing causing minor confusion. Did not fully brief the examinee as to the conduct and purpose of the evaluation. **(T-3)**

4.4.2.3. U. Examiner failed to adequately brief the examinee. **(T-3)**

4.4.3. AREA 24, Performance Assessment and Grading (M)

4.4.3.1. Q. Identified all discrepancies and assigned proper area grade. **(T-3)**

4.4.3.2. Q-. Most discrepancies were identified. Failed to assign Q- grade when appropriate. Assigned discrepancies for performance which was within standards. **(T-3)**

4.4.3.3. U. Failed to identify discrepancies related to mission discipline or deviations which merited an unqualified grade. Assigned Q- grades that would have been U or assigned U grades for performance within standards. **(T-3)**

4.4.4. AREA 25, Assessment of Overall Performance (M).

4.4.4.1. Q. Awarded the appropriate overall grade based on the examinee's performance. **(T-3)**

4.4.4.2. Q-. Awarded an overall grade without consideration of cumulative deviations in the examinee's performance. **(T-3)**

4.4.4.3. U. Did not award a grade commensurate with overall performance. **(T-3)**

4.4.5. AREA 26, Assignment of Additional Training (M).

4.4.5.1. Q. Assigned proper additional training if warranted and briefed the individual's training officer. *NOTE:* If the QUAL Examinee's performance (i.e. Q1) does not warrant the assignment of additional training, the SEE Examinee will verbally explain to the SEE Examiner the proper procedures for assigning additional training. This may be accomplished as part of the SEE Objectivity pre-brief or debrief. **(T-3)**

4.4.5.2. Q-. Additional training assigned was insufficient to ensure the examinee would achieve proper level of qualification. **(T-3)**

4.4.5.3. U. Failed to assign additional training when warranted and/or failed to brief the individual's training officer. **(T-3)**

4.4.6. AREA 27, Mission Critique (M).

4.4.6.1. Q. Thoroughly debriefed the examinee and supervisor on all aspects of the evaluation. Debriefed all key mission events, providing instruction and references as required. **(T-3)**

4.4.6.2. Q-. Failed to discuss all deviations and assigned grades. Did not advise the examinee of additional training, if required. Failed to debrief or adequately reconstruct all key mission events. **(T-3)**

4.4.6.3. U. Did not discuss any assigned area grades or the overall rating. Changed grades without briefing the examinee. Did not debrief any portion of the mission. Debriefed few or no key mission events. **(T-3)**

4.5. SEE Objectivity Evaluation Documentation. SEE Objectivity Evaluations will be documented as a SPOT evaluation on the AF Form 4418 and AF Form 4420 and maintained in the member's cyber crew qualification folder IAW AFI 17-202 Vol 2 and applicable higher headquarters/local supplemental guidance. **(T-3)**

4.5.1. Letter of Xs.

4.5.1.1. Upon the successful completion of a SEE Objectivity Evaluation, units will ensure the crewmembers' SEE status is reflected on the Letter of Certifications. **(T-3)**

4.5.1.2. Upon the decertification or loss of SEE qualification, units will ensure the Letter of Certifications appropriately reflects the crewmember's status. **(T-3)**

WILLIAM J. BENDER, Lt Gen, USAF
Chief of Information Dominance and
Chief Information Officer

Attachment 1

GLOSSARY OF REFERENCES AND SUPPORTING INFORMATION

References

AFPD 17-2, *Cyberspace Operations*, 12 April 2016

AFI 17-202V1, *Cybercrew Training*, April 2, 2014

AFI 17-202V2, *Cybercrew Standardization and Evaluation*, October 15, 2014

AFI 17-202V3, *Cyberspace Operations Procedures*, May 6, 2015

AFI 33-360, *Publications and Forms Management*, 18 May 2006

AFMAN 33-363, *Management of Records*, 1 March 2008

Adopted Forms

AF Form 847, *Recommendation for Change of Publication*

Abbreviations and Acronyms

AF—Air Force

AFI—Air Force Instruction

ACD—Air Force Cyberspace Defense

AFMAN—Air Force Manual

AFPD—Air Force Policy Directive

AFRC—Air Force Reserve Command

AFSPC—Air Force Space Command

ANG—Air National Guard

CCC—Crew Commander

COMSEC—Communications Security

EAP—Emergency Action Procedures

EPE—Emergency Procedure Evaluation

HQ—Headquarters

IAW—In Accordance With

INSTR— Instructor

MAJCOM—Major Command

MISUM—Mission Summary

MSL—Master Station Log

MSN—Mission Qualification

AFI17-2NASV2 10 FEBRUARY 2017

NAF—Numbered Air Force

N/N—No-notice

OC—Operations Controller

OG—Operations Group

OG/CC—Operations Group Commander

OGV—Operations Group Standardization/Evaluation

OPR—Office of Primary Responsibility

OPSEC—Operational Security

QUAL—Qualification

SEE—Stan/Eval Examiner

SPOT—Spot Evaluation

SQ—Squadron

STAN/EVAL—Standardization and Evaluation

Terms

ACD-O—Cyberspace operator qualified to perform Air Force Cyber Defense (ACD) Operator duties.

Airmanship—A crew member's continuous perception of self and weapon system/mission equipment in relation to the dynamic environment of operations, threats, and tasking, and the ability to forecast and execute tasks based on that perception.

Commendable—An observed exemplary demonstration of knowledge and/or or noteworthy ability to perform by the examinee in a particular graded area/subarea, tactic, technique, procedure, and/or task.

Crew Commander (CCC)—Cyberspace operator qualified to perform crew commander duties.

Deficiency—Demonstrated level of knowledge or ability to perform is inadequate, insufficient, or short of meeting required or expected proficiency.

Deviation—Performing an action not in sequence with current procedures, directives, or regulations. Performing action(s) out of sequence due to unusual or extenuating circumstances is not considered a deviation. In some cases, momentary deviations may be acceptable; however, cumulative deviations will be considered in determining the overall qualification level.

Discrepancy—Any observed deviations/errors/omissions, individually or cumulative, that detracts from the examinee's performance in obtaining a Q for a particular grading area/subarea.

Error—Departure from standard procedure. Performing incorrect actions or recording inaccurate information.

Stan/Eval Examiner (SEE—)—A crew member designated to administer evaluations.

Inadequate—Lack or underutilization of available crew aids or resources to effectively/efficiently make operational and tactical decisions, gain/maintain situational awareness, or accomplish a task.

Inappropriate—Excessive reliance on crew aids/other resources or utilizing a crew aid/resource outside its intended use.

Instructor—Crew member trained, qualified, and certified by the squadron commander as an instructor to perform crew training.

Instructor Supervision—When a current instructor, who is qualified in the same crew position, supervises a maneuver or training event.

Letter of X's—This document serves as the commander's tool to track specialized training. The letter of x's is not a source document for certifications and qualifications; it is a display of information found in the source documents.

Major (deviation/error/omission)—Detracted from task accomplishment, adversely affected use of equipment, or violated safety.

Minor (deviation/error/omission)—Did not detract from task accomplishment, adversely affect use of equipment, or violate safety.

Omission—The leaving out of a required action or annotation.

Operations Controller (OC)—Cyberspace operator qualified to perform operations controller duties.

Supervised Training Status—Crew member will perform weapon system duties under instructor supervision as designated by the squadron commander or evaluator.

BY ORDER OF THE
SECRETARY OF THE AIR FORCE

AIR FORCE INSTRUCTION 17-2NAS
VOLUME 3

10 FEBRUARY 2017

Cyberspace

NETWORK ATTACK SYSTEM (NAS)
OPERATIONS AND PROCEDURES

COMPLIANCE WITH THIS PUBLICATION IS MANDATORY

ACCESSIBILITY: Publications and forms are available for downloading or ordering on the e-Publishing website at www.e-publishing.af.mil.

RELEASABILITY: There are no releaseability restrictions on this publication.

OPR: AF/A3CO/A6CO

Certified by: AF/A3C/A6C
(Brig Gen Kennedy)
Pages: 21

This volume implements Air Force (AF) Policy Directive (AFPD) 17-2, Cyberspace Operations; AFI 17-202V1, *Cybercrew Training,* AFI 17-202V2, *Standardization/Evaluation,* and AF Instruction (AFI) 17-202 V3, *Cyberspace Operations and Procedures*. It applies to all units which operate the NAS. This publication applies to all military and civilian AF personnel, members of the AF Reserve Command (AFRC), Air National Guard (ANG), and contractor support personnel in accordance with appropriate provisions contained in memoranda support agreements and AF contracts.

The authorities to waive wing/unit level requirements in this publication are identified with a Tier ("T-0, T-1, T-2, T-3") number following the compliance statement. See AFI 33-360, Publications and Forms Management, Table 1.1 for descriptions of the authorities associated with the Tier numbers. Submit requests for waivers through the chain of command to the appropriate Tier waiver approval authority, or alternately, to the Publication Office of Primary Responsibility (OPR) for non-tiered compliance items. Refer recommended changes and questions about this publication to the OPR using the AF Form 847, *Recommendation for Change of Publication*; route AF Form 847s from the field through Major Command (MAJCOM) publications/forms managers to AF/A3C/A6C. Ensure all records created as a result of processes prescribed in this publication are maintained in accordance with AF Manual (AFMAN) 33-363, *Management of Records* and disposed of in accordance with the AF Records Disposition Schedule (RDS) located in the AF Records Management Information System (AFRIMS).

Chapter 1

GENERAL GUIDANCE

1.1. General. This volume, in conjunction with other governing directives, prescribes procedures for operating the NAS weapon system under most circumstances. It is not a substitute for sound judgment or common sense. Procedures not specifically addressed may be accomplished if they enhance safe and effective mission accomplishment.

1.2. References, Abbreviations, Acronyms, and Terms. See Attachment 1.

1.2.1. For the purpose of this instruction, "certification" denotes a commander's action, whereas qualification denotes a formal Standardization/Evaluation (Stan/Eval) evaluation.

1.2.2. Key words explained.

1.2.2.1. "Will," "Must," or "Shall" indicate a mandatory requirement.

1.2.2.2. "Should" indicates a preferred, but not mandatory method of accomplishment.

1.2.2.3. "May" indicates an acceptable or suggested means of accomplishment.

1.2.2.4. "Note" indicates operating procedures, techniques, etc, which are considered essential to emphasize.

1.2.2.5. "Normally" indicates under normal or usual conditions; as a rule.

1.3. Waivers. Unless another approval authority is cited, waiver authority for this volume is AF Space Command (AFSPC)/A2/3/6T. Forward waiver requests through appropriate channels to the AFSPC/A2/3/6T for approval. All approvals will include an expiration date. Waivers are issued for a maximum of one year from the effective date.

1.4. Deviations. In the case of an urgent requirement or emergency the Crew Commander (CCC) will take appropriate action(s) to ensure safe operations. **(T-3)**

1.5. Processing Changes.

1.5.1. Submit recommended changes and questions about this publication through MAJCOM channels to the OPR per Technical Order (TO) 00-5-1, *AF Technical Order System*, using AF Form 847, *Recommendation for Change of Publication*. **(T-2)**

1.5.2. The submitting MAJCOM will forward information copies of AF Forms 847 to all other MAJCOMS that use this publication. Using MAJCOMs will forward comments on AF Forms 847 to the OPR. **(T-2)**

1.5.3. The OPR will:

1.5.3.1. Coordinate all changes to the basic instruction with affected MAJCOM/A3s. **(T-2)**

1.5.3.2. Forward change recommendations to MAJCOM/A3 for staffing and AF/A3 approval. **(T-2)**

1.6. Supplements. Guidance for supplementing this publication is contained in AFI 33-360, *Publications and Forms Management.* Supplements will not duplicate, alter, amend or be less restrictive than the provisions of this Instruction. **(T-2)**

Chapter 2

MISSION PLANNING

2.1. Responsibilities. Individual crew members, unit operations, and theater intelligence functions jointly share responsibility for mission planning. The CCC is ultimately responsible for all tactical aspects of mission planning to include complying with command guidance. Unit commanders may supplement mission planning requirements but will ensure an appropriate level of mission planning is conducted prior to each mission.

2.2. Mission Planning Guidelines.

2.2.1. Effective mission accomplishment requires thorough mission planning and preparation. Specific mission planning elements are addressed in Air Force Tactics, Techniques, and Procedures (AFTTP) 3-1.*General Planning*, AFTTP 3-1.NAS, Air Force Cyber Command (AFCYBER) & Joint Forces Headquarters-Cyber (JFHQ-C) AFCYBER Tactical Mission Planning, Briefing and Debriefing Guide, and any local crew aids. While not directive, these manuals are authoritative and useful in ensuring adequate mission planning and employment.

2.2.2. Standard Operating Procedures (SOP). The Squadron Commander (SQ/CC) is the approval authority for squadron standards. Operations Group Commander (OG/CC) may publish and approve group standards. The operations group Stan/Eval office (OGV) will review all standards for compliance with AFI 17-series guidance. **(T-3)**

2.2.3. Units will accomplish sufficient planning to ensure successful mission accomplishment. Units will maintain facilities where all information and materials required for mission planning are available. **(T-3)**

2.2.4. Commanders will ensure that crews have sufficient time and resources to accomplish mission planning and briefing, and that non-mission critical activities do not interfere with the time allotted for mission planning and briefing. **(T-3)**

2.3. Master Station Log (MSL).

2.3.1. The MSL is the unit's official record of events that occurred during operations. The purpose is to maintain an accurate and detailed record of all significant events pertaining to operations occurring during each sortie. The CCC is responsible for documenting significant events/crew actions required for the MSL **(T-3)**. As a minimum, required items are:

2.3.1.1. Tasking Order. **(T-3)**

2.3.1.2. Crew line-up. **(T-3)**

2.3.1.3. Mission Fires. **(T-3)**

2.3.1.4. Crew Information Files. **(T-3)**

2.3.1.5. Changes to Mission Materials. **(T-3)**

2.3.1.6. Status of the Weapon System. **(T-3)**

2.4. Briefings.

2.4.1. CCC is responsible for presenting a briefing to promote safe and effective missions. All crew members will attend the mission brief unless they have previously coordinated their absence with Squadron Director of Operations (SQ/DO). **(T-3)**

2.4.2. CCC will plan adequate time to discuss required briefing items depending on complexity of the missions and operator capabilities. **(T-3)**

2.4.2.1. Any item published in MAJCOM/Numbered Air Force (NAF)/wing/group/squadron standards or AFIs and understood by all participants may be briefed as "standard".

2.4.3. Briefing Guides. Briefing guides will be used by the lead briefer with a reference list of items which may apply to particular missions. Briefing Guide can be found in Attachment 2. Units may augment these guides as necessary. Items may be briefed in any sequence; provided all minimum requirements listed in this AFI and other local directives and guidance are addressed. **(T-3)**

2.4.4. Anyone not attending the mission brief will receive, as a minimum, an overview of the mission objectives, their roles and responsibilities and emergency procedures (EP) upon arriving for duty **(T-3)**.

2.4.5. Positional Changeover Brief. Positional changeover briefings with the oncoming crew will be delivered in accordance with (IAW) checklist(s) and applicable directives. CCCs are responsible for specifically briefing any ongoing missions at changeover and/or any missions that will roll into the next crew duty period (12 hours). **(T-3)**

Chapter 3

NORMAL OPERATING PROCEDURES

3.1. Pre-Mission Arrival Times. The CCC, in coordination with the DO, may adjust crew report time to meet mission requirements. Crew report times will allow sufficient time to mentally and physically prepare for duty. **(T-3)**

3.1.1. Mission Planning Cell (MPC). If a MPC is utilized, the SQ/DO or MPC Chief (MPCC) will set the show time. **(T-3)**

3.2. Mission Duties. While on duty, CCCs will ensure that conducting operations takes precedence over any other activities/events on the operations floor. **(T-3)**

3.3. Go/No-Go. CCCs are responsible for implementing Go/No-Go procedures IAW the latest version of the 624th Operations Center (624 OC) Standing Special Instructions (SPINS) and other local directives and guidance. **(T-3)**

3.3.1. At a minimum, the unit Go/No-Go process will verify the following for all crew members, to include instructors and evaluators, scheduled to perform crew duties:

3.3.1.1. Qualification/certification of each scheduled crew member IAW AFI 17-2NAS Volumes 1 and 2 for the crew position and mission they are scheduled to perform duties. Note: Crew members not qualified/certified and in training status will require instructor or evaluator supervision to conduct crew duties. **(T-3)**

3.3.1.2. Currency and proficiency of each scheduled crew member IAW AFI 17-2NAS Volume 1 for the crew position and mission for they are scheduled to perform duties. Note: Crew members not current in the crew position and/or mission will require instructor supervision to conduct crew duties until regaining currency. **(T-3)**

3.3.1.3. Currency of each crew member on the review of CIFs. Note: Mission Management software tracks and updates the status of new CIFs. Crew members will read new CIFs before being checked in for crew duties by the CCC in the Mission Management software. **(T-3)**

3.4. Crew Information File (CIF)/ Read Files. Crew members will review CIFs and Read Files before all missions, and update the CIF currency record via Mission Management software. **(T-3)**

3.4.1. Items in the Read File may include local procedures and policies concerning equipment and personnel generally not found in any other publications. **(T-3)**

3.5. Unit-Developed Checklists/Local Crew Aids.

3.5.1. Locally developed checklists and crew aids will be used and will, as a minimum, include the following **(T-3)**:

3.5.1.1. Emergency action checklists and communication-out information. **(T-3)**

3.5.1.2. Position-specific weapon system employment information as deemed necessary by the unit. **(T-3)**

3.5.2. Unit Stan/Eval will maintain the listing of current and authorized checklists, crew aids, etc. **(T-3)**

3.6. Required Equipment/Publications. All crew members will have all required equipment and publications required for mission execution. Some publications may be maintained and carried electronically provided operable viewing and printing capability exists throughout mission execution. Unit Standards & Evaluations will maintain the list of required items. **(T-3)**

3.7. Operations Check (Ops Check). Accomplish sufficient ops checks to ensure safe and effective mission accomplishment(s). **(T-3)**

3.7.1. Operations Technicians will perform Ops Checks at initial check-in and as required during sortie period based on mission triggers and requirements. **(T-3)**

3.8. Vulnerability/Mission Window. Crews are bounded by the mission window. Deviations from the assigned window will be coordinated through the CCC and approved by 624 OC/COD and/or the tasking authority. **(T-3)**

3.9. Abort/Knock-it-off. A CCC, Authorized Initiator or 624 OC/COD may declare a knock-it-off (training use only) or abort (cease action/event/mission). **(T-3)**

3.10. Dynamic Targeting. Ad hoc and/or "on call" tasking can occur. These taskings are initiated by Authorized Initiators and communicated to the crews IAW currently published 624 OC Standing SPINS. **(T-3)**

3.11. Communications and Crew Coordination. Recorded crew communications are official communications, and crews should be aware they have no expectation of privacy. **(T-3)**

3.11.1. Sterile Ops Floor. Official communications channels will be limited to conversations essential for mission coordination and accomplishment. **(T-3)**

3.11.2. Advisory Calls. The operator performing the execution will announce their intentions during the critical checkpoints/phases of operations and when circumstances require deviating from normal procedures. **(T-3)**

3.11.3. Common brevity codes can be found in the current 624 OC Standing SPINs. **(T-3)**

3.11.4. Communications.

3.11.4.1. The communication plan will be employed IAW currently published 624 OC Standing SPINS. **(T-3)**

3.11.4.2. The CCC is responsible for briefing the communication plan. **(T-3)**

3.12. Mission Summary (MISUM). Crew Commander is responsible for providing timely, accurate, and correctly formatted reports to tasking authority. **(T-3)**

3.12.1. A MISUM will be accomplished once the cybercrew has completed the tasking order IAW currently published 624 OC Standing SPINs and locally-developed procedures. **(T-3)**

3.12.2. The CCC is responsible for reviewing the MISUM for accuracy and completeness and submission to tasking authority. **(T-3)**

3.12.3. Local procedures/templates may be developed to ensure standardization of reporting. **(T-3)**

3.13. Crew Changeover. In order to validate the readiness of both the crew and system, the off-going CCC or Operations Controller will conduct a shift change briefing at changeover. All required duty positions will be present for the briefing. **(T-3)**

3.14. Debriefing.

3.14.1. All missions will be debriefed at all levels required. **(T-3)**

3.14.2. The CCC is responsible for leading the crew debrief, all crew members will be present to participate. **(T-3)**

3.14.3. Debriefs will cover all aspects of the mission (planning, briefing and execution) and ensure all participants receive feedback through the development of Lessons Learned (LL) and Learning Points (LP). **(T-3)**

3.14.4. CCC will review the record of all tactical portions of the sortie to assess members' effectiveness. **(T-3)**

3.14.5. Debriefing guide can be found in Attachment 3.

3.15. Post Mission Duties.

3.15.1. Each crew member will complete any additional tasks deemed necessary by the CCC in relation to the current mission. **(T-3)**

3.15.2. Ops Floor Cleanliness. It is the CCC and/or Crew Non-Commissioned Officer In-Charge's responsibility to ensure the ops floor is clean and orderly after a mission. All crew members are responsible for removing or stowing their personal and professional items prior to departing the floor. **(T-3)**

Chapter 4

CREW DUTIES, RESPONSIBILITIES, AND PROCEDURES

4.1. Crew Commander (CCC) Responsibilities. The CCC is responsible for each sortie, and for the safe, effective conduct of operations. Crew members are responsible to the CCC for the successful accomplishment of all activities. CCC responsibilities and/or authority include:

4.1.1. Managing crew resources and safe mission accomplishment. **(T-3)**

4.1.2. Welfare of crew members. **(T-3)**

4.1.3. Ensuring that any portion of the operation affecting the accomplishment of the mission is coordinated with the tasking authority. **(T-3)**

4.1.4. Ensuring risk management decision matrix is performed when tasking(s) is received. **(T-3)**

4.2. Crew Stations. Crew members shall be in their seats on the operations floor during the critical checkpoints/phases of execution. Crew members will notify the CCC prior to departing their assigned primary duty station. **(T-3)**

4.3. Crew Duties. Crew members are responsible for successful sortie completion, and for the safe, effective use of the weapon system. A crew brief will be accomplished at the start of the crew duty period and before each sortie as necessary to ensure an understanding of all aspects of the mission(s). **(T-3)**.

4.4. Crew Positions.

4.4.1. NAS Crew Commander (CCC). Serves as the command authority for NAS crew operations and is responsible for execution and monitoring of all operations and is the unit's focal point for mission tasking from the tasking authority. The CCC is responsible for the review, approval and execution of all operations under his/her purview.

4.4.2. NAS Operations Controller (OC). Serves as the tactical authority for NAS crew operations and is responsible for mission planning, execution and mission monitoring for all missions built and fired under his/her purview.

4.4.3. NAS Operator (CO). The NAS Operator is qualified to conduct all NAS missions. Is responsible for the accuracy and timeliness of any mission assigned by the CCC/Operations Controller and is responsible for mission monitoring IAW unit best practices.

4.5. Crew Manning. Mission manning may vary by the type of mission; SQ/DO may tailor crew manning to meet operational requirements. Minimum crew complement: 1x Crew Commander, 1x Operations Controller, 2x Cyberspace Operators, 1x Operations Technician. **(T-3)**

4.5.1. No more than ten (10) simultaneous missions per Crew Commander/Operations Controller unless waived by the 624 OC/SDO IAW 624 OC Standing SPINS. **(T-3)**

4.6. Crew Qualification. Each person assigned as a primary crew member will be qualified in that crew position. Those crew members in a training status will accomplish weapon system operations and/or positional duties only under the supervision of a qualified instructor. **(T-3)**

4.6.1. Combat Mission Ready (CMR) crew members may perform primary crew duties in any position in which they maintain certification, currency, and proficiency. **(T-3)**

4.6.2. In supervised status, crew members may perform crew duties only under the supervision of a qualified instructor/evaluator. Non-current crew members may regain currency after performing crew duties under the supervision of a qualified crew member. There are no Basic Mission Capable (BMC) positions associated with the NAS. **(T-3)**

4.7. New/Modified Equipment and/or Capabilities. Crew members not qualified and/or certified in the operation of new or modified equipment and/or weapon system capabilities will not operate that equipment unless under the supervision of a qualified instructor of like specialty. **(T-3)**

4.8. Crew Rest/Duty Period/Sortie Duration. Crew rest, crew duty period, and crew augmentation will be IAW all applicable guidance with the following additional guidance:

4.8.1. Crew Rest. Crew rest is a minimum 10-hour non-duty period before the duty period begins to ensure the crew member is adequately rested before performing a mission or mission-related duties. Crew rest is free time that allows time for meals, transportation, and rest. Rest is defined as a condition that allows an individual the opportunity to sleep. Each crew member is individually responsible for ensuring they obtain sufficient rest during crew rest periods. **(T-3)**

4.8.2. Exceptions to the 10-Hour Minimum Crew Rest Period. The crew rest exception shall only be used for contingency/surge operations and not for scheduling conveniences. **(T-3)**

4.8.3. Duty Period. The normal crew duty period is twelve (12) hours. **(T-3)**

4.8.4. Sortie. For planning purposes, the average cybercrew sortie duration (ASD) is two (2) hours. Each line item in the published Tasking Order is a NAS sortie. Reference 624 OC Standing SPINS for more planning/tasking information. **(T-3)**

4.9. Crew Scheduling. Scheduling mission crew members will be accomplished IAW crew rest limitations provided in this AFI. Units will make every effort to ensure compliance. **(T-3)**

4.9.1. Units will attempt to provide all crew members as stable a schedule as possible. A standard rotation for 24/7 crew members should be utilized to enhance performance. **(T-3)**

4.9.2. Schedulers will publish, post, and monitor schedules for the crew force and initiate changes to the schedules based on proper tracking of qualifications, certifications, restrictions and other factors as required to meet mission objectives. **(T-3)**

Chapter 5

LARGE FORCE EMPLOYMENT

5.1. Mission Planning. Individual crew members, unit operations, and theater intelligence functions jointly share responsibility for mission planning. The Task Force, Campaign Planners or Non-Kinetic Duty Officer is ultimately responsible for effectively integrating the NAS into theater operations, to include complying with command guidance. Effective mission accomplishment requires thorough mission planning and preparation. Failures in execution are often indicative of poor mission preparation. **(T-3)**

5.2. Briefing. NAS CCC will receive relevant mission employment guidance from the tasking organization in order to support the tactical plan. **(T-3)**

5.3. Debriefing. The NAS CCC will ensure the Mission Commander (MC) or designated tasking organization receives relevant outputs from the crew debrief. Additionally, if required, the CCC or designated alternate can attend a mission debrief. **(T-3)**

5.4. Arrival Times. If an MPC is utilized the Mission Planning Cell Chief (MPCC) sets show time for crew members. **(T-3)**

5.5. Roles and Responsibilities. The tactical situation may dictate the organization and roles of the MPC. All or some of the roles may be in other squadrons. **(T-3)**

5.5.1. Mission Planning Cell Chief (MPCC). Proactively leads all aspects of the planning process. Approves detailed timeline based on overall mission-planning time and tasks to be accomplished. Designates personnel to track time (timekeeper), record discussions (scribe) and update master copy of plan/objectives (slide person). The MPCC will designate a deputy mission planning cell chief (DMPCC) and package commanders (PC) if necessary. **(T-3)**

5.5.2. Mission Commander (MC). Responsible for all mission related forces assigned in the tasking order. The MC will plan in conjunction with the Mission Planning Cell Chief (MPCC), coordinate, lead, and debrief the mission. MC delegates aspects of mission planning in order to create sufficient detail in the allotted timeframe. **(T-3)**

5.5.3. Package Commander (PC). PC responsible for understanding how the tactical problem set relates to their package. PC communicates package capacities and limitations, capacities and planning requirements. PC will coordinate across all units that are capable of employing tasks for specified package. PC will deconflict efforts and dependencies with other Package Commanders. PC will determine how the specified package can mutually support another package. PC will provide planning updates to local unit(s) leadership on employment of package. **(T-3)**

5.5.4. Intelligence, Surveillance, and Reconnaissance (ISR) Lead. Will brief threats to mission success. Will submit/answer ISR related requests for information. **(T-3)**

5.6. Mission Go/No-Go Criteria. Proper go/no-go criteria identified during mission planning improve decision making and allow the MC, CC, PC, etc. to make rational and timely decisions regarding mission execution. **(T-3)**

WILLIAM J. BENDER, Lt Gen, USAF
Chief of Information Dominance and
Chief Information Officer

Attachment 1

GLOSSARY OF REFERENCES AND SUPPORTING INFORMATION

References

AFPD 17-2, *Cyberspace Operations,* 12 April 2016

AFI 17-202V1, *Cybercrew Training*, April 2, 2014

AFI 17-202V2, *Cybercrew Standardization and Evaluation*, October 15, 2014

AFI 17-202V3, *Cyberspace Operations Procedures*, May 6, 2015

AFI 33-360, *Publications and Forms Management*, 25 September 2013

TO 00-5-1 *AF Technical Order System*

AFTTP 3-1.NAS

AFCYBER & JFHQ-C AFCYBER Tactical Mission Planning, Briefing and Debriefing Guide

AFTTP 3-1.General Planning

AFTTP 3-1.Threat Guide Chapter 13

624 Operations Center Standing SPINS

Adopted Forms

AF Form 847, *Recommendation for Change of Publication*

AFTO Form 781, *ARMS Crew/Mission Data Document*

Abbreviations and Acronyms

AF—Air Force

AFPD—Air Force Policy Directive

AFI—Air Force Instruction

AFMAN—Air Force Manual

AFRC—Air Force Reserve Command

AFRIMS—Air Force Records Information Management System

AFSPC—Air Force Space Command

AFTTP—Air Force Tactics, Techniques and Procedures

ANG—Air National Guard

ASD—Average Sortie Duration

BMC—Basic Mission Capable

CC—Commander

CCC—Crew Commander

CIF—Crew Information File

CMR—Combat Mission Ready

CT—Continuation Training

DO—Director of Operations

DMPCC—Deputy Mission Planning Cell Chief

EP—Emergency Procedures

IAW—In Accordance With

ISR—Intelligence, Surveillance, and Reconnaissance

JFHQ-C—Joint Forces Headquarters-Cyber

LL—Lesson Learned

LP—Learning Point

MAJCOM—Major Command

MC—Mission Commander

MISUM—Mission Summary

MPC—Mission Planning Cell

MPCC—Mission Planning Cell Chief

MR—Mission Ready

NAF—Numbered Air Force

NAS—Network Attack System

OG—Operations Group

OGV—Standardization and Evaluation

OPR—Office of Primary Responsibility

PC—Package Commander

RDS—Records Disposition Schedule

SOP—Standard Operating Procedures

SPINS—Special Instructions

SQ—Squadron

USAF—United States Air Force

Terms

Authorized Initiator—Individual(s) authorized by Combatant Commanders to execute specific mission(s).

Average Sortie Duration (ASD)—ASD is used to convert sorties to flying/execution hours and vice versa. MAJCOM/A3TB uses the unit's last programmed ASD when initially determining execution/flying hour's programs for the current and future years. Units will update ASD annually to reflect the unit's best estimate of the optimum sortie duration after considering historical experiences, changes in missions, deployments, etc. The formula to calculate ASD is ASD = # of weapon system hours employed divided by number of sorties.

Basic Mission Capable (BMC)—The status of a crew member who has satisfactorily completed IQT and MQT to perform the unit's basic operational missions, but does not maintain Mission Ready (MR)/CMR status. Crew member accomplishes training required to remain familiarized in all and may be qualified and proficient in some of the primary missions of their weapon system BMC requirements. These crew members may also maintain special mission qualification.

Campaign—A series of related major operations aimed at achieving strategic and operational objectives within a given time and space.

Certification—Designation of an individual by the certifying official as having completed required training and/or evaluation and being capable of performing a specific duty.

Combat Mission Ready (CMR)—A crew member who has satisfactorily completed IQT and MQT, and maintains certification, currency and proficiency in the command or unit combat mission.

Continuation Training (CT)—Training which provides crew members with the volume, frequency, and mix of training necessary to maintain currency and proficiency in the assigned qualification level.

Crew Commander (CCC)—Serves as the command authority for NAS operations and provides command oversight for operations floor personnel as well as enforcing policies and procedures to ensure successful mission accomplishment.

Crew Information File (CIF)—A collection of publications and material determined by the MAJCOM and unit as necessary for day-to-day operations.

Crew Position Indicator (CPI)—Codes used to manage crew positions to ensure a high state of readiness is maintained with available resources.

Crew—The personnel and positions necessary to conduct cyberspace sorties. A NAS crew must be composed of the minimum required personnel defined in this document.

Crew member—Individuals who conduct cyberspace operations or computer network exploitation and are typically assigned to a specific weapon system.

Currency—A measure of how frequently and/or recently a task is completed. Currency requirements should ensure the average crew member maintains a minimum level of proficiency in a given event.

Cyber (adj.)—Of or pertaining to the cyberspace environment, capabilities, plans, or operations.

Cyberspace Operations (CO)—The employment of cyberspace capabilities where the primary purpose is to achieve objectives in or through cyberspace.

Cyberspace—A global domain within the information environment consisting of the interdependent network of information technology infrastructures and resident data, including the Internet, telecommunications networks, computer systems, and embedded processors and controllers.

Cyberspace Crew Commander-Attack (CCC-A)—Serves as the command authority for NAS crew operations and is responsible for execution and monitoring of all operations and is the unit's focal point for mission tasking from the tasking authority. The CCC is responsible for the review, approval and execution of all operations under his/her purview.

Cyberspace Operations Controller-Attack (OC-A)—Serves as the tactical authority for NAS crew operations and is responsible for mission planning, execution and mission monitoring for all missions built and fired under his/her purview.

Cyberspace Operations Technician-Attack (OT-A)—Responsible for the efficient operation of the weapon system as well as correct configurations of the system based on tasked operations. Only crew member authorized to troubleshoot system errors or resolve system deficiencies.

Cyberspace Operator-Attack (CO-A)—Qualified to execute any NAS mission. Is responsible for the accuracy and timeliness of any mission assigned by the CCC/Operations Controller and is responsible for mission monitoring IAW unit best practices.

Deviation—Performing action(s) not in sequence with current procedures, directives, or regulations. Performing action(s) out of sequence due to unusual or extenuating circumstances is not considered a deviation. In some cases, momentary deviations may be acceptable; however, cumulative deviations will be considered in determining the overall qualification level.

Event—An item that occurs or is encountered that initiates a process requiring a set of tasks to be accomplished. Multiple events may be completed and logged during a sortie (be it operational sortie or a training sortie) unless specifically excluded elsewhere in this instruction.

Instructor—An experienced individual qualified to instruct other individuals in mission area academics and positional duties. Instructors will be qualified appropriately to the level of the training they provide.

Mission—Missions are operations conducted with an intended purpose. Missions are conducted by a unit and/or units with relevant capability and preponderance of capacity.

Mission Ready—A crew member who has satisfactorily completed IQT and MQT, and maintains certification, currency and proficiency in the command or unit operational mission.

Mission Window—This is a window of opportunity and direction for a tactical commander to conduct operations. A Mission Window is bounded (start by/finish by) to give a tactical commander the authorized and suspense timing available to plan and prosecute mission. Deviations from the assigned Mission Window will be approved by the tasking authority.

Qualification—Designation of an individual by the unit commander as having completed required training and evaluation and being capable of performing a specific duty.

Ready Cybercrew Program (RCP)—RCP is the formal continuation training (CT) program that provides the baseline for squadrons to use in developing a realistic training program to meet all DOC statement tasked requirements as well as specific NAF mission prioritization. RCP defines the minimum required mix of annual sorties, simulator missions, and training events crew members must accomplish to sustain mission readiness. These programs have clearly defined objectives and minimum standard that enhance mission accomplishment and safety. RCP sorties are tracked. In order to be effective, each mission must successfully complete a sufficient number of events applicable to that mission type, as determined by the squadron commander. With completion of IQT and MQT, a crew member is trained in all the basic missions of a specific unit, unless a specific exception is provided in the weapon system-specific 17-2 Vol 1.

Sortie—The actions an individual weapon system takes to accomplish missions and/or mission objectives within a defined start and stop period.

Supervised Status—The status of a crew member who must perform missions under the supervision of an instructor.

Target—The adversary.

Task—A clearly defined action or activity specifically assigned to an individual or organization that must be done as it is imposed by an appropriate authority.

Upgrade Training—Training needed to qualify to a crew position of additional responsibility for a specific weapon system (e.g., special mission qualifications).

Weapon System—A combination of one or more weapons with all related equipment, materials, services, personnel, and means of delivery and deployment (if applicable) required for self-sufficiency.

Attachment 2

BRIEFING

This attachment provides guidance and consideration for developing unit briefing guides. Additional guidance and information can be found in the Air Force Tactics, Techniques, and Procedures (AFTTP) 3-1.General Planning, AFTTP 3-1.NAS, AFCYBER & JFHQ-C AFCYBER Tactical Mission Planning, Briefing and Debriefing Guide, and others. These manuals are authoritative not directive and should be considered when developing unit specific guides.

Note: This layout can be used for multiple briefs; however, the focus areas and emphasis items will be different as the audiences are different.

1.   Timehack

2.   Objectives

3.   Tasks to Meet Objectives

4.   Assessment Plan

5.   Timeline

6.   Resource Assignments

7.   Constraints/Restraints

8.   Assumptions/Contingencies

9.   Comm Plan / C2 Plan

10.   Admin

11.   Questions / Comments

Attachment 3

DEBRIEF

Debrief Presentation Format:

1.   Reconstruction

2.   Assess Mission Accomplishment

3.   Debrief Focal Points

4.   Root Cause Analysis

5.   Lessons Learned/Learning Points

Cybersecurity Titles Published by 4th Watch Publishing Co.

NIST SP 500-288	Specification for WS-Biometric Devices (WS-BD)
NIST SP 500-291 V2	NIST Cloud Computing Standards Roadmap
NIST SP 500-292	NIST Cloud Computing Reference Architecture
NIST SP 500-293 V1 & V2	US Government Cloud Computing Technology Roadmap
NIST SP 500-293 V3	US Government Cloud Computing Technology Roadmap
NIST SP 500-299	NIST Cloud Computing Security Reference Architecture
NIST SP 500-304	Data Format for the Interchange of Fingerprint, Facial & Other Biometric Information
NIST SP 800-12 R1	An Introduction to Information Security
NIST SP 800-16 R1	A Role-Based Model for Federal Information Technology/Cybersecurity Training
NIST SP 800-18 R1	Developing Security Plans for Federal Information Systems
NIST SP 800-22 R1a	A Statistical Test Suite for Random and Pseudorandom Number Generators for Cryptographic Applications
NIST SP 800-30	Guide for Conducting Risk Assessments
NIST SP 800-31	Intrusion Detection Systems
NIST SP 800-32	Public Key Technology and the Federal PKI Infrastructure
NIST SP 800-34 R1	Contingency Planning Guide for Federal Information Systems
NIST SP 800-35	Guide to Information Technology Security Services
NIST SP 800-36	Guide to Selecting Information Technology Security Products
NIST SP 800-37 R2	Applying Risk Management Framework to Federal Information
NIST SP 800-38	Recommendation for Block Cipher Modes of Operation
NIST SP 800-38A Addendum	Block Cipher Modes of Operation: Three Variants of Ciphertext Stealing for CBC Mode
NIST SP 800-38B	Block Cipher Modes of Operation: The CMAC Mode for Authentication
NIST SP 800-38C	Block Cipher Modes of Operation: The CCM Mode for Authentication and Confidentiality
NIST SP 800-38D	Block Cipher Modes of Operation: Galois/Counter Mode (GCM) and GMAC
NIST SP 800-38E	Block Cipher Modes of Operation: The XTS-AES Mode for Confidentiality on Storage Devices
NIST SP 800-38F	Block Cipher Modes of Operation: Methods for Key Wrapping
NIST SP 800-38G	Block Cipher Modes of Operation: Methods for Format-Preserving Encryption
NIST SP 800-39	Managing Information Security Risk
NIST SP 800-40 R3	Guide to Enterprise Patch Management Technologies
NIST SP 800-41	Guidelines on Firewalls and Firewall Policy
NIST SP 800-44 V2	Guidelines on Securing Public Web Servers
NIST SP 800-45 V2	Guidelines on Electronic Mail Security
NIST SP 800-46 R2	Guide to Enterprise Telework, Remote Access, and Bring Your Own Device (BYOD) Security
NIST SP 800-47	Security Guide for Interconnecting Information Technology Systems
NIST SP 800-48	Guide to Securing Legacy IEEE 802.11 Wireless Networks
NIST SP 800-49	Federal S/MIME V3 Client Profile
NIST SP 800-50	Building an Information Technology Security Awareness and Training Program
NIST SP 800-52 R1	Guidelines for the Selection, Configuration, and Use of Transport Layer Security (TLS) Implementations
NIST SP 800-53 R5	Security and Privacy Controls for Information Systems and Organizations
NIST SP 800-53A R4	Assessing Security and Privacy Controls
NIST SP 800-54	Border Gateway Protocol Security
NIST SP 800-56A R3	Pair-Wise Key-Establishment Schemes Using Discrete Logarithm Cryptography
NIST SP 56B R 1	Recommendation for Pair-Wise Key-Establishment Schemes Using Integer Factorization Cryptography
NIST SP 800-56C R1	Recommendation for Key-Derivation Methods in Key-Establishment Schemes - Draft
NIST SP 800-57 R4	Recommendation for Key Management
NIST SP 800-58	Security Considerations for Voice Over IP Systems
NIST SP 800-60	Guide for Mapping Types of Information and Information Systems to Security Categories
NIST SP 800-61 R2	Computer Security Incident Handling Guide
NIST SP 800-63-3	Digital Identity Guidelines
NIST SP 800-63a	Digital Identity Guidelines - Enrollment and Identity Proofing
NIST SP 800-63b	Digital Identity Guidelines - Authentication and Lifecycle Management
NIST SP 800-63c	Digital Identity Guidelines- Federation and Assertions
NIST SP 800-64 R2	Security Considerations in the System Development Life Cycle
NIST SP 800-66	Implementing the Health Insurance Portability and Accountability Act (HIPAA) Security Rule
NIST SP 800-67 R2	Recommendation for Triple Data Encryption Algorithm (TDEA) Block Cipher - Draft
NIST SP 800-70 R4	National Checklist Program for IT Products
NIST SP 800-72	Guidelines on PDA Forensics
NIST SP 800-73-4	Interfaces for Personal Identity Verification
NIST SP 800-76-2	Biometric Specifications for Personal Identity Verification
NIST SP 800-77	Guide to IPsec VPNs
NIST SP 800-79-2	Authorization of Personal Identity Verification Card Issuers (PCI) and Derived PIV Credential Issuers (DPCI)
NIST SP 800-81-2	Secure Domain Name System (DNS) Deployment Guide
NIST SP 800-82 R2	Guide to Industrial Control Systems (ICS) Security
NIST SP 800-83	Guide to Malware Incident Prevention and Handling for Desktops and Laptops
NIST SP 800-84	Guide to Test, Training, and Exercise Programs for IT Plans and Capabilities
NIST SP 800-85A-4 PIV	Card Application and Middleware Interface Test Guidelines
NIST SP 800-85B-4 PIV	Data Model Test Guidelines - Draft
NIST SP 800-86	Guide to Integrating Forensic Techniques into Incident Response

NIST SP 1800-4a & 4b Mobile Device Security: Cloud and Hybrid Builds
NIST SP 1800-4c Mobile Device Security: Cloud and Hybrid Builds
NIST SP 1800-5 IT Asset Management: Financial Services
NIST SP 1800-6 Domain Name Systems-Based Electronic Mail Security
NIST SP 1800-7 Situational Awareness for Electric Utilities
NIST SP 1800-8 Securing Wireless Infusion Pumps
NIST SP 1800-9a & 9b Access Rights Management for the Financial Services Sector
NIST SP 1800-9c Access Rights Management for the Financial Services Sector - How To Guide
NIST SP 1800-11a & 11b Data Integrity Recovering from Ransomware and Other Destructive Events
NIST SP 1800-11c Data Integrity Recovering from Ransomware and Other Destructive Events - How To Guide
NIST SP 1800-12 Derived Personal Identity Verification (PIV) Credentials
NISTIR 7298 R2 Glossary of Key Information Security Terms
NISTIR 7316 Assessment of Access Control Systems
NISTIR 7497 Security Architecture Design Process for Health Information Exchanges (HIEs)
NISTIR 7511 R4 V1.2 Security Content Automation Protocol (SCAP) Version 1.2 Validation Program Test Requirements
NISTIR 7628 R1 Vol 1 Guidelines for Smart Grid Cybersecurity - Architecture, and High-Level Requirements
NISTIR 7628 R1 Vol 2 Guidelines for Smart Grid Cybersecurity - Privacy and the Smart Grid
NISTIR 7628 R1 Vol 3 Guidelines for Smart Grid Cybersecurity - Supportive Analyses and References
NISTIR 7756 CAESARS Framework Extension: An Enterprise Continuous Monitoring Technical Refer
NISTIR 7788 Security Risk Analysis of Enterprise Networks Using Probabilistic Attack Graphs
NISTIR 7823 Advanced Metering Infrastructure Smart Meter Upgradeability Test Framework
NISTIR 7874 Guidelines for Access Control System Evaluation Metrics
NISTIR 7904 Trusted Geolocation in the Cloud: Proof of Concept Implementation
NISTIR 7924 Reference Certificate Policy
NISTIR 7987 Policy Machine: Features, Architecture, and Specification
NISTIR 8006 NIST Cloud Computing Forensic Science Challenges
NISTIR 8011 Vol 1 Automation Support for Security Control Assessments
NISTIR 8011 Vol 2 Automation Support for Security Control Assessments
NISTIR 8040 Measuring the Usability and Security of Permuted Passwords on Mobile Platforms
NISTIR 8053 De-Identification of Personal Information
NISTIR 8054 NSTIC Pilots: Catalyzing the Identity Ecosystem
NISTIR 8055 Derived Personal Identity Verification (PIV) Credentials (DPC) Proof of Concept Research
NISTIR 8060 Guidelines for the Creation of Interoperable Software Identification (SWID) Tags
NISTIR 8062 Introduction to Privacy Engineering and Risk Management in Federal Systems
NISTIR 8074 Vol 1 & Vol 2 Strategic U.S. Government Engagement in International Standardization to Achieve U.S. Objectives for Cybersecurity
NISTIR 8080 Usability and Security Considerations for Public Safety Mobile Authentication
NISTIR 8089 An Industrial Control System Cybersecurity Performance Testbed
NISTIR 8112 Attribute Metadata - Draft
NISTIR 8135 Identifying and Categorizing Data Types for Public Safety Mobile Applications
NISTIR 8138 Vulnerability Description Ontology (VDO)
NISTIR 8144 Assessing Threats to Mobile Devices & Infrastructure
NISTIR 8151 Dramatically Reducing Software Vulnerabilities
NISTIR 8170 The Cybersecurity Framework
NISTIR 8176 Security Assurance Requirements for Linux Application Container Deployments
NISTIR 8179 Criticality Analysis Process Model
NISTIR 8183 Cybersecurity Framework Manufacturing Profile
NISTIR 8192 Enhancing Resilience of the Internet and Communications Ecosystem
Whitepaper Cybersecurity Framework Manufacturing Profile
Whitepaper NIST Framework for Improving Critical Infrastructure Cybersecurity
Whitepaper Challenging Security Requirements for US Government Cloud Computing Adoption
FIPS PUBS 140-2 Security Requirements for Cryptographic Modules
FIPS PUBS 140-2 Annex A Approved Security Functions
FIPS PUBS 140-2 Annex B Approved Protection Profiles
FIPS PUBS 140-2 Annex C Approved Random Number Generators
FIPS PUBS 140-2 Annex D Approved Key Establishment Techniques
FIPS PUBS 180-4 Secure Hash Standard (SHS)
FIPS PUBS 186-4 Digital Signature Standard (DSS)
FIPS PUBS 197 Advanced Encryption Standard (AES)
FIPS PUBS 198-1 The Keyed-Hash Message Authentication Code (HMAC)
FIPS PUBS 199 Standards for Security Categorization of Federal Information and Information Systems
FIPS PUBS 200 Minimum Security Requirements for Federal Information and Information Systems
FIPS PUBS 201-2 Personal Identity Verification (PIV) of Federal Employees and Contractors
FIPS PUBS 202 SHA-3 Standard: Permutation-Based Hash and Extendable-Output Functions

DHS Study DHS Study on Mobile Device Security

OMB A-130 / FISMA OMB A-130/Federal Information Security Modernization Act
GAO Federal Information System Controls Audit Manual

DoD	
UFC 3-430-11	Boiler Control Systems
UFC 4-010-06	Cybersecurity of Facility-Related Control Systems
FC 4-141-05N	Navy and Marine Corps Industrial Control Systems Monitoring Stations
MIL-HDBK-232A	RED/BLACK Engineering-Installation Guidelines
MIL-HDBK 1195	Radio Frequency Shielded Enclosures
TM 5-601	Supervisory Control and Data Acquisition (SCADA) Systems for C4ISR Facilities
ESTCP	Facility-Related Control Systems Cybersecurity Guideline
ESTCP	Facility-Related Control Systems Ver 4.0
DoD	Self-Assessing Security Vulnerabilities & Risks of Industrial Controls
DoD	Program Manager's Guidebook for Integrating the Cybersecurity Risk Management Framework (RMF) into the System Acquisition Lifecycle
DoD	Advanced Cyber Industrial Control System Tactics, Techniques, and Procedures (ACI TTP)
DoD 4140.1	Supply Chain Materiel Management Procedures
AFI 17-2NAS	Air Force Network Attack System (NAS) Volume 1, 2 & 3
AFI 10-1703	Air Force Cybercrew Volume 1, 2 & 3
AFI 17-2ACD	Air Force Cyberspace Defense (ACD) Volume 1, 2 & 3
AFI 17-2CDA	Air Force Cyberspace Defense Analysis (CDA) Volume 1, 2 & 3
AFPD 17-2	Cyberspace Operations